How To Achieve Professional Excellence

Unleashing Your Potential through Strategic Skill Development

SKILLSETS FOR SUCCESS – BOOK 2

DR. K. V. SAHASRANAM MD.   DM. FACC.

ABOUT THE AUTHOR

Dr. K. V. Sahasranam (Sahasranam Kalpathy) is the author of ten books previously on various subject like He has been practicing as a Senior Consultant Cardiologist in a multispecialty hospital in India and was the Chief of Medical Services there.

His books of Short Stories are named **'Tell Me A Story, Grandpa'** and **'Grandpa, Tell Me More Stories.'** His third book **'In Search of a Bridegroom'** is an Autobiographical fiction based on his first-hand experiences. Two books in a series dealing with the Health Problems of Elderly persons are **'How to face the Health Challenges While Growing Old'** and **'Old Age Health – Challenges and Solutions.'** **'Understanding the Electrocardiogram'** is a handbook for doctors, medical residents, and nurses. His book **'Demystifying Hinduism'** describes the Basics of Hinduism in a Q & A format. His second book, , is **'The Avadhoota – Whispers of Wisdom'.** The book **"*Daily Musings*"** is the third book

The first book in the series 'Skillsets for Success' was named **"How to Master Essential Life Skills"**. He has described more skills needed to be successful in life in this book.

He is a retired Cardiologist settled in the U.S.

Dedication

To my Teachers

in school and college, who ignited the flames of knowledge within me, I offer my heartfelt gratitude.

Your guidance and wisdom have shaped my academic journey in ways beyond measure.

This book stands as a tribute to your unwavering dedication and invaluable influence on my education.

TABLE OF CONTENTS

ACKNOWLEDGEMENT

I wish to express my sincere gratitude to Dr. K. G. Alexander, Chairman and Managing Director of Baby Memorial Hospital. In my role as Chief of Medical Services and Senior Consultant in Cardiology, his guidance has proven invaluable in navigating complex situations in the hospital.

Special thanks are due to Ms. Gracy Mathai, CEO of Baby Memorial Hospital. Her unwavering support and mentorship were crucial during my tenure, and her management expertise played a pivotal role in honing my leadership skills for overseeing a large group of doctors and residents.

My gratitude extends to Mr. Saji Mathew, the hospital's COO, for his multifaceted role in managing the IT and HR departments. His inspiration and guidance in leadership and management principles significantly contributed to my role as Chief of Medical Services.

I extend my thanks to the members of the Hospital Management Committee for their consistent support, as there was always something to learn from each of them.

Throughout my management tenure, insights were gleaned not only from top leaders but also from fellow doctors, nurses, managers, residents, and other staff across various departments. Their collective contributions played a pivotal role in the successful completion of my term as Medical Director.

The inspiration for this book was drawn from diverse sources such as library books, podcasts, YouTube videos, TED talks, and blogs. I sincerely thank the authors of these mediums for their valuable contributions.

A special mention goes to my family, whose unwavering support was indispensable during the challenging process of authoring this book. Their encouragement served as a constant source of strength and motivation, and I acknowledge their pivotal role in this endeavor.

I also want to extend my thanks to Mr. Som Bathla, my mentor on this authorial journey, and the supportive members of the Author-Helping-Author (AHA) community. Their constructive suggestions at various stages of writing and publishing have been invaluable.

I would also like to place on record my appreciation of the services rendered by Ms. Lolitha of Revandesigns in designing a beautiful cover for this book.

COPYRIGHT

Copyright © 2024 by Dr. K. V. Sahasranam. All rights reserved. No part of this book may be produced or stored in a retrieval system or transmitted in any form by any means, electronic, photocopying, recording, or otherwise, without express written permission of the author.

DISCLAIMER

The information presented in the book, including facts and statistics, is sourced from reliable and authentic references. The book conveys the author's personal suggestions and opinions. Notably, the author has made a conscientious effort to safeguard the identities of individuals involved in real incidents from his career. These incidents are cited solely for illustrative purposes and not with the intent to disparage any individual or institution. Names have been changed wherever needed to ensure anonymity.

PREFACE

This is the second book in the *"Skillsets for Success"* series, following the initial one release titled **"How to Master Essential Life Skills."** The preceding book delved into common skills crucial for professional advancement. In this volume, I aim to explore additional professional skills essential for success in both life and career.

Within these pages, I expound upon key skills pertinent to hospital employees. While not exclusively tailored for doctors and nurses, this discourse encompasses all non-medical hospital staff, appealing to a diverse audience, including general readers, students, teachers, and even humble homemakers seeking personal development.

Several pivotal skills, including *Team Management, Leadership Qualities, Feedback and Criticism, Coaching and Mentoring,* and *Mastering Meetings,* are indispensable for professional success. Additionally, skills like *Attitude* and *Anger Management* form integral aspects of daily human interaction across various life spheres.

I introduce a novel skill, *Management by Wandering Around,* emphasizing its utility in specific situations. In the healthcare context, the importance of *Medical Ethics* extends to doctors, nurses, and other medical professionals.

Throughout this book, I share anecdotal instances requiring diplomatic navigation, drawn from my experiences, both pre and post my tenure in a private multispecialty hospital. My previous experiences while teaching in the Medical College at Calicut, India also has greatly contributed to my experience. My journaling background aids in chronicling these experiences, with names and designations altered for anonymity preservation.

I trust this humble effort will prove valuable to all hospital staff and healthcare professionals. I urge readers to critically evaluate the book and provide candid opinions. Such frank reviews will motivate further contributions to the "*Skillsets for Success*" series.

With these words, I present my book to you, dear readers.

Dr. K. V. Sahasranam.

INTRODUCTION

"In Book-1 of the series, "Skillsets for Success" we explored various crucial soft skills. This volume further delves into additional skills, imperative for success in effectively interacting with and managing people. Whether you are a manager, employee, student, self-employed professional, or housewife, these skills are essential. The omitted skills from the previous book are now covered.

Among the most crucial soft skills for career success are Leadership and Team Management. The chapter dedicated to Mastering Meetings comprehensively addresses the indispensable elements required to convene and conduct successful meetings in any organization.

This book caters to employees and middle-level managers across diverse industries. It's crucial to understand that skills are not innate; they evolve through continuous training and practice. Those neglecting skill development risk lagging behind in their careers, with diminished prospects for advancement.

While the book is situated in a healthcare organization context, the outlined skills are equally applicable to non-medical employees, doctors, and nurses. They are universal, suitable for individuals in any industry.

Students, academics, teachers, and housewives can all derive benefits from the skills presented. Coaching and mentoring play vital roles in enhancing productivity and the overall working environment within any organization."

Feedback and criticism are equally vital for a homemaker managing school-going children as they are for the CEO of a multinational corporation. Unchecked anger can lead to disastrous consequences, a topic explored in the section on Anger Management. A person's attitude is the defining characteristic, particularly in organizational settings, where it significantly influences individual success.

Every office requires effective management of its front office. Hence, a comprehensive chapter on Front Office Management outlines the essential qualities of an efficient receptionist. This book delves into these principles in considerable detail.

Managing By Wandering Around, a novel management concept, holds equal or greater importance in healthcare settings. A dedicated chapter on Medical Ethics addresses the ethical dilemmas faced by healthcare professionals, including doctors, nurses, and other staff. This book aims to guide healthcare providers and employees, offering valuable insights. While not a comprehensive management guide, it proves beneficial for those lacking formal skill management training, such as employees, middle-level managers, and supervisors.

Interacting with patients and their families is integral to healthcare duties, extending from the front desk receptionist to doctors, nurses, technicians, and other staff. Healthcare professionals, ranging from medical students to nurses, must possess skills to navigate diverse patient backgrounds, cultures, and attitudes. This necessitates patience and resilience, coupled with emotional intelligence. This book provides tips and guidance to assist readers in refining their people management skills."

1. Inspire, Lead, Succeed - LEADERSHIP & MOTIVATION

*"Management is doing things right.
Leadership is doing the right things."*
—Peter Drucker

Leadership is not an innate trait; it is cultivated. Leadership skills encompass qualities, knowledge, abilities, and behaviors enabling an individual to guide, coach, and inspire others toward a shared objective. These skills are indispensable for executives, empowering them to make decisions aligned with the organization's mission and vision.

Regardless of one's position in the organizational hierarchy—whether a CEO, manager, supervisor, or project leader—the role of a leader carries significant responsibility. A leader must motivate subordinates to unleash their full potential through dedicated efforts. Additionally, instilling an inspiring vision is crucial for fostering team motivation. Setting well-defined goals is a pivotal aspect of this motivational process.

Decisiveness, trustworthiness, resilience, team empowerment, and clear communication skills are fundamental prerequisites for effective leadership.

Distinguishing Between Leadership and Management

A manager primarily oversees the tasks performed by their staff, ensuring successful completion without consistently prioritizing employee motivation or team inspiration. Their focus lies in achieving organizational goals efficiently, emphasizing control, supervision, and the maintenance of continuous operations.

On the contrary, a leader serves to inspire and motivate followers and employees within the organization, going beyond mere management. Their decision-making is geared towards motivating employees to attain the organization's objectives. A leader acts as a role model, making decisions aligned with the organization's values and vision, prompting members to willingly follow. Intrinsic motivation is instilled by a leader, and the acknowledgment and praise they provide instill confidence and pride among the organization's employees.

While a leader can also function as a manager, not every manager possesses the qualities of a leader. *A leader is necessarily a manager, but a manager is not always a leader*. Leadership requires special skills and talents, setting it apart from the more generalized role of a manager.

QUALITIES OF AN EFFECTIVE LEADER

Certain skills are essential for a leader to possess. Let us briefly examine what these skills entail.

Communication: A successful leader must excel in communication, encompassing both verbal and non-verbal aspects. Proficiency in these skills is vital to motivate and inspire followers. Clarity and confidence are key when speaking, with careful consideration of words and phrases relevant to the context. Great leaders often incorporate short parables, stories, and anecdotes into their speeches for inspiration. Public speaking is a mastered skill for effective leaders, ensuring every conversation serves a specific objective. Even non-verbal cues exude motivational elements, displaying a decisive, purposeful, and confident communication style. Leaders adeptly communicate with the right people at the right time and in the right manner.

Active listening is integral to communication. Leaders dedicate more time to listening than speaking to subordinates, fostering an understanding that enables motivation. Maintaining eye contact and employing appropriate gestures and responses further enhance their communication skills.

Empathy: Empathy is a crucial trait for effective leadership. A skilled leader understands the importance of demonstrating empathy at the right moments. This involves expressing genuine concern for the well-being of employees and followers, going the extra mile to understand their personal lives, hobbies, family dynamics, and other interests. A true leader engages in informal conversations with the team that don't revolve around work or the organization. Moreover, they actively participate in personal celebrations such as birthdays, weddings, baby showers, and other events, fostering a sense of familial connection.

Indeed, an authentic leader views all team members as part of an 'extended family.' This mindset contributes to a supportive and cohesive work environment. Beyond emotional well-being, a leader takes concrete steps to ensure the comfort and safety of employees within the office. This includes providing facilities for recreation and fitness. Offering wellness activities and on-site amenities such as a gym and a childcare facility exemplify this warm-hearted approach. By creating a workplace that prioritizes the holistic well-being of its members, a leader cultivates a positive and thriving organizational culture.

Zeal: Positivity stands as a crucial trait for any leader. A proficient leader consistently directs attention towards the positive facets of a situation, even in the presence of unfavorable elements. Maintaining a positive attitude and a pleasant demeanor, their mere presence cultivates a sense of happiness among team members. The leader actively opts for the use of 'optimistic' language, avoiding negative expressions in their communication. Through consistent encouragement, praise, and due recognition, a leader fosters motivation within the team.

Integrity: Integrity and honesty are essential qualities of an exemplary leader. The conduct and demeanor of a commendable leader consistently reflect their core values. An exceptional leader upholds ethical standards and demonstrates unwavering loyalty to their followers, earning both respect and affection. Transparency characterizes their communication, as they candidly present facts to employees without concealment.

A noteworthy leader displays respect for others, cultivating reciprocal respect from those surrounding them. Prioritizing the welfare of followers over personal interests, a commendable leader remains attentive to their concerns. Fairness and impartiality define their actions, free from bias or hypocrisy. Adhering strictly to elevated ethical standards, they anticipate the same commitment from followers and employees alike.

Reliability: A dependable leader consistently provides steadfast support to their team, fostering genuine reliance on their decisions. Punctuality is a hallmark trait, demonstrated through timely attendance at meetings and other sessions. This leader places a premium on others' time, exemplifying organizational standards. Their reliability extends to consistently yielding results and adeptly managing crises. Dependability and trustworthiness remain enduring qualities.

A trustworthy leader consistently honors commitments, viewing task completion and goal achievement as matters of pride. They respect and adhere to deadlines while remaining adaptable when circumstances require flexibility.

Motivation: A proficient leader endeavors to inspire and motivate employees, steering organizational change and fostering transformation. Methods encompass recognizing and appreciating staff, empowering them with responsibilities, cultivating a positive work environment, and offering abundant opportunities for skill development and career growth. The leader strives to cultivate a workplace culture that promotes collaboration, respect, and mutual trust among employees.

Promoting a proper work-life balance is crucial for sustaining employee motivation and encouraging optimal performance. The leader tailors motivation approaches based on individual preferences, attitudes, and personalities, contributing to a workplace culture that nurtures creativity, innovation, and commitment to continuous improvement.

Motivated employees, drawing inspiration from the leader's words, remain focused on organizational goals. The leader prioritizes addressing employees' health needs by promoting well-being through annual health checkups, vaccinations, a balanced diet, and appropriate recreational activities.

The leader emphasizes intrinsic motivation for self-development and career progression, avoiding demotivation by providing recognition and rewards. Increasing intrinsic motivation involves setting challenging goals, ensuring fair treatment, and providing positive feedback, fostering an optimistic attitude among employees and propelling them toward success in their endeavors.

Goal Setting: A leader motivates his team by establishing SMART goals. Both individuals and organizations must define precise objectives to ensure ongoing development. Leaders work closely with employees and executives to formulate SMART goals, leveraging the talent within the organization's resource pool. They remain receptive to ideas during goal setting and impartially embrace them.

Open to Ideas: Embracing ideas and constructive criticism without bias is a vital trait for any leader. Simultaneously, a leader should not shy away from providing constructive feedback to his team members. This cooperative mindset fosters the growth and prosperity of the organization. Every member of the organizational hierarchy, regardless of their position, has the opportunity to offer feedback and suggestions. The leader, in turn, impartially accepts and implements them if they benefit the organization or its employees. This open-minded approach instills confidence in the workforce.

Conflict Handling: A proficient leader adeptly manages conflicts within their organization with effectiveness and impartiality, steering clear of any bias when addressing internal disputes. The leader actively engages with both parties involved, attentively listening to their concerns and devising solutions that are agreeable to all. In doing so, they uphold organizational decorum without sacrificing interpersonal relationships among employees. Employing a collaborative conflict resolution approach, the leader ensures that the proposed solutions are acceptable to all conflicting parties. A skilled leader is vigilant, identifying conflicts early and promptly intervening to facilitate resolution, preventing them from escalating. (See Chapter on *'Conflict Resolution'* in Book 1).

Personal Improvement: In addition to supporting the training and development of his team, a true leader dedicates time to enhance his own skills and broaden his knowledge. He possesses self-awareness regarding his limitations and demonstrates the ability to prioritize effectively. Consequently, he actively engages in self-development and acquires new skills, with a primary focus on tackling fresh challenges and advancing the organization.

An effective leader also excels as a mentor. Investing time and effort into the growth of team members, he hones the necessary skills to be an exemplary mentor. This involves refining communication and time management skills to stay current with the times, leveraging these abilities for the advancement of the organization.

Furthermore, a proficient leader embraces change, particularly in the face of technological advancements, and stays abreast of trends in management and business. With self-discipline, a leader inspires confidence among employees, fostering an environment conducive to achieving ambitious goals and enhancing overall productivity.

Perseverance: A proficient leader adeptly confronts impediments to progress and surmounts them to attain success. This ability enables leaders to confront challenges, persist in their pursuit of goals, and prevail against unfavorable circumstances. When leaders introduce changes, they often encounter obstacles that demand resilience for successful implementation and positive organizational transformation. A commendable leader rarely succumbs to quitting, upholding a resolute mindset grounded in moral and ethical principles when facing challenges and hindrances to progress. Employees appreciate a leader's persistence, as it fosters an environment of sustained effort and unwavering commitment.

President Trump, in 2018, exhibited remarkable persistence, compelling North Korean leader Kim Jong Un to engage in negotiations despite formidable resistance. This resolute approach resulted in a historic meeting in Singapore, showcasing the President's decisive leadership. Leaders who firmly believe in the righteousness of their actions persistently pursue their objectives, undeterred by opposition and criticism. They persevere in doing what they deem right, ultimately achieving their planned goals.

Leaders who think that what they are doing is right are a persistent lot and achieve what they plan to do. In spite of opposition and criticism, they press on to do what they feel is right.

Team Building: Collaboration and teamwork stand out as key attributes of an effective leader. Such a leader consistently promotes team-building activities and takes a proactive role in leading the team. Moreover, the leader never overlooks the importance of celebrating the accomplishments of team members, fostering a positive team culture.

A proficient leader actively urges team members to engage in collaborative efforts, enhancing both performance and morale within the team. Recognizing the unique strengths and talents of each team member, a good leader assigns appropriate roles within the department to optimize functionality. This leader involves the team in activities, skills development, and problem-solving-oriented team-building exercises.

Serving as the driving force behind the team, the leader instills a sense of unity by encouraging strong interpersonal relationships among team members. Through dedicated team-building exercises, a resilient bond is forged among the members, ultimately contributing to the overall strength and cohesion of the team.

Delegation: A leader effectively assigns tasks to team members based on their skills and confidence in their abilities. When delegating a task, the leader grants authority while also sharing responsibility for its successful completion. This approach ensures that crucial tasks are completed on time, empowering team members to independently carry out their assigned responsibilities. Consequently, team members experience increased satisfaction and trust, boosting their morale. Through consistent delegation, the leader mentors them for future leadership roles.

Delegation serves as a valuable tool for reducing employee burnout and lowering attrition rates within the organization. A leader who entrusts responsibilities to their team members builds trust and respect, leading to enhanced efficiency and heightened productivity in the organization

VARIOUS LEADERSHIP STYLES

Leadership styles signify the manner in which a leader conducts themselves when guiding a group. Researchers have categorized these into seven distinct types [4]. Several styles are elucidated below, accompanied by examples.

1. **Autocratic Leadership:** This approach involves the leader autonomously making all decisions, asserting control and authority over the team. Clear instructions on what, how, and when tasks are to be executed are provided. This proves advantageous in situations requiring prompt

24

decision-making, particularly during crises. Example: Jeff Bezos, the founder of Amazon.

2. **Democratic Leadership:** In contrast to the aforementioned style, democratic leadership incorporates all members in the decision-making process through active collaboration and participation. Also known as the *'Participative Style,'* it proves highly effective. Leaders employing this style provide guidance to their members while simultaneously considering and valuing their input and suggestions on crucial decisions. This inclusive approach fosters a sense of involvement and motivation among the members. An exemplary figure demonstrating democratic leadership is Sundar Pichai, the CEO of Google.

3. **Transformational Leadership:** These leaders empower their team members to realize and attain their full potential, inspiring them through adept communication. For instance, figures like Elon Musk, the CEO of Tesla and SpaceX, Asim Premji of Wipro, and Sanjiv Bajaj of Bajaj Finserv epitomize this leadership style.

4. **Transactional Leadership:** Leaders adopting this approach not only inspire and motivate their team members but also exhibit emotional intelligence and zeal for their objectives. They employ a reward and punishment system, contingent on performance and accomplishments, within the framework of a well-defined employer-employee relationship accompanied by monetary benefits. Roles for both the leader and the team members are explicitly outlined, fostering clear expectations. Nevertheless, it's important to note that this leadership style tends to stifle creativity. Prominent examples include Mary Barra, the

CEO of General Motors, and business magnates such as Ratan Tata and Mukesh Ambani.

5. **Charismatic Leadership:** The term implies a leader possessing a captivating personality that draws in and inspires followers. Such leaders utilize articulate communication to propel their members towards action and goal attainment. Their alluring personalities serve as a source of inspiration and influence for their teams. Notable examples include Richard Branson, the founder of the Virgin Group, as well as Mahatma Gandhi and Martin Luther King.

6. **Relationship-Oriented Leadership:** Leaders following this approach establish robust connections with their team members. They actively engage in the well-being and personal growth of their team. A notable example is Satya Nadella, the CEO of Microsoft.

7. **Situational Leadership :** This type involves leaders adjusting their approach according to particular demands and emerging circumstances. Tim Cook, Apple's CEO, exemplifies this adaptability.

Leaders frequently find it necessary to tailor their leadership style to the specific characteristics of the organization they oversee and the individuals within their team. There are instances when the leader must modify their leadership style to address the current needs effectively. Nevertheless, despite these situational adjustments, the fundamental mode of operation generally remains consistent across various leaders.

Leaders frequently find it necessary to tailor their leadership style to the specific characteristics of the organization they oversee and the individuals within their team. There are instances when the leader must modify their leadership style to address the current needs effectively. Nevertheless, despite these situational adjustments, the fundamental mode of operation generally remains consistent across various leaders.

In conclusion, the dynamic interplay of leadership and motivation emerges as the catalyst for organizational success, as effective leaders inspire and empower individuals to achieve their highest potential. As we conclude this chapter, it is evident that true leadership goes hand in hand with the art of motivation, creating a synergy that propels teams towards shared goals and fosters a culture of continuous growth. To encapsulate our exploration of leadership and motivation, it becomes clear that great leaders not only guide teams but also ignite the flame of inspiration, transforming challenges into opportunities and individuals into a motivated, high-performing collective.

"A leader is one who knows the way, goes the way and shows the way." — John C. Maxwell

---

2. Navigating Group Dynamics - TEAM MANAGEMENT

"There is no elevator to success; you have to take the stairs." — Zig Ziglar

In the contemporary world, there is a growing recognition of unexpected changes. As a result, managers must transition from *'just in time'* management to *'just in case'* management to effectively respond to these unforeseen developments. The core of team management revolves around the attainment of organizational goals. Team managers need to concentrate on the day-to-day execution of tasks, ultimately leading to the successful achievement of the organization's objectives. A proficient team manager should skillfully organize the team to coordinate the activities of its members and foster a sense of camaraderie and collaboration among them.

Modern-day employees seek acknowledgment. Within an organization, it is imperative for the workforce to derive a sense of purpose from their tasks. A competent team manager should motivate team members to align with these objectives. In a study conducted in the United States, 1300 CEOs from various companies were queried about essential employee skills for effective team management. Leadership, Adaptability, Soft Skills, Problem Solving, Creativity, and Innovation emerged as crucial qualities. Human attributes were prioritized over technology and hard skills, highlighting the undeniable truth that human imagination cannot be replaced by an algorithm.

Team management is defined as an individual's or an organization's ability to coordinate and oversee a group of people in the pursuit of a common task. The effectiveness of team management is crucial for enhancing efficiency, productivity, and collaboration among team members. Furthermore, it fosters a sense of job satisfaction, empowering and valuing team members. It plays a pivotal role in the training and development of team members, preparing them for higher roles within the organization.

As a result, a team manager must possess essential skills to keep team members motivated towards achieving the organization's goals. Essentially, every team leader is a leader in their own right and requires leadership qualities.

Let's briefly explore some of the necessary attributes for becoming a successful team manager.

Communication: In leadership and team management alike, effective communication is paramount. A proficient team manager excels in both verbal and non-verbal communication. A successful team leader not only conveys management decisions and expectations clearly but also motivates team members to efficiently pursue organizational goals within specified timeframes. During meetings, the leader must adeptly address raised issues and guide conversations with timely interventions. Transparency in sharing information vital for organizational growth is crucial, establishing a communication bridge between management and employees.

Additionally, a competent team manager is a keen listener. Practicing active listening, the manager values input from every team member, regardless of their position. Given the diverse personalities and attitudes within a team, effective communication is essential for fostering camaraderie and preventing conflicts.

Conflict Resolution: Conflicts frequently arise within teams. Paradoxically, these conflicts can serve as a catalyst for the team, opening up new avenues and giving rise to fresh ideas and creative content. They also provide insights into the diverse strengths and weaknesses of team members. Hence conflicts need not necessarily be considered undesirable. Conflicts hence may indirectly contribute to increased productivity within the organization.

However, conflicts can become detrimental if not appropriately addressed in a timely manner. Allowing conflicts to persist is never advisable, and it falls upon the team manager to ensure their amicable resolution. A proficient team manager must possess the skill of adept conflict management, resolving disputes without causing harm to either party involved.

The adept team manager is capable of finding a "win-win" solution – one that is mutually acceptable to both parties. Proactively recognizing and resolving disputes before they escalate into serious conflicts is a hallmark of effective conflict management.

Delegation: Delegation is a crucial skill for an effective team manager. To delegate tasks successfully, the manager must have the trust of their team members. It is essential to identify the right person for the job before assigning responsibilities. Each team member possesses unique skills and competencies, making it crucial to delegate tasks to individuals based on their talents. Delegating involves entrusting not only the task itself but also the responsibility and accountability for its completion within the specified deadline.

Once a task is delegated, the manager should refrain from micromanaging the team member responsible for it. This approach fosters confidence in the employee and builds trust. In essence, effective delegation empowers the team, leveraging individual strengths and ensuring tasks are handled with expertise and efficiency.

Flexibility: A team manager needs to exhibit flexibility by recognizing the unique capabilities of individual team members and adapting to them. The allocation of work should be personalized based on their abilities and skills. Moreover, a manager should be open-minded and receptive to novel ideas and suggestions from the team, fostering a positive relationship. Being approachable and maintaining pleasant interactions with all team members is crucial for building trust in the team leader.

Furthermore, a competent team manager must demonstrate a willingness to learn new skills and stay updated on the latest technology. Adaptability and openness to change are essential traits. Initiating changes in the team's functioning when necessary to enhance efficiency is a key responsibility for a manager.

Growth and Development: The team manager ought to actively engage in the growth and development of team members, affording them every chance to progress within the organization. It is imperative for the manager to identify the strengths and weaknesses of each team member, guiding them effectively to enhance their careers. Encouraging team members to evolve and acquire new skills beneficial to their careers is crucial. Providing training and growth opportunities is a responsibility inherent in every team manager's role. Additionally, the manager should support the aspirations and goals of team members, ensuring their best interests are prioritized. The cultivation of a culture that fosters polite and respectful freedom of expression within the team should also be promoted.

Discipline: Every team comprises individuals with diverse personalities, and it becomes the responsibility of the team leader to discern these differences and adapt their approach, accordingly, considering the distinct personalities and idiosyncrasies of each member. It is imperative for the team leader to instill discipline within the team, taking into account the varying attitudes and temperaments of its members. This involves ensuring adherence to principles such as telephone etiquette, punctuality, meeting deadlines, proper conduct during meetings, and fostering positive interpersonal relationships.

Furthermore, the team leader must oversee proper grooming practices to prevent any conflicts of interest within the team. When a team member's attitude or behavior poses a threat to the team's cohesion or violates organizational rules, decisive action may be required. The team leader should possess the ability to address such misdemeanors efficiently and diplomatically.

Establishing benchmarks for the group and implementing clear rules is essential to avoid chaos and conflicts within the team. These measures contribute to a cohesive and well-functioning team, where members can collaborate harmoniously towards common goals.

Objectivity: It is crucial for a team leader to maintain impartiality and objectivity in their approach. Personal sentiments and biases must not obscure their judgment or interactions with team members. Only by doing so can team members place trust and confidence in the leader. Additionally, the leader should possess the ability to regulate their emotions and maintain self-awareness regarding their role within the organization.

> *The hospital's Medical Committee, comprising department chiefs, convened monthly, chaired by the medical director. These sessions were conducted with decorum, adhering to principles of team management. Department chiefs actively engaged, offering constructive suggestions and improvement ideas. Amid the pandemic, meetings transitioned to virtual platforms, maintaining robust participation and interaction. Feedback often used to be given regarding various departments and their performance to the Chiefs in an atmosphere of camaraderie and collaboration*

Training and Development: A manager should possess the ability to identify potential areas of improvement in individual team members and facilitate their training for future development, benefiting both the individual and the organization. It is crucial to concentrate on the strengths of each team member, providing targeted training to enhance their skills. Investing in the development of team members yields advantages for both employees and the organization.

Within a team, members exhibit diverse temperaments and outlooks. Some may require guidance and 'handholding' to meet deadlines, while others operate independently and efficiently. For those who may be lagging in their tasks, a manager should offer motivation and encouragement to help them accomplish their responsibilities.

The manager's responsibility extends to providing resources and management support for essential soft skills training and updating technological proficiency among employees. Encouraging participation in conferences, educational programs, and workshops can significantly improve their skills. Simultaneously, the team manager should take a proactive approach to update and develop his own skills.

Feedback & Criticism: Constructive feedback plays a crucial role in the success of any team. Studies indicate that employees tend to perform better and enhance their efficiency when they receive feedback. It becomes the responsibility of the team leader to consistently provide positive and constructive feedback to team members, fostering encouragement and support. This practice cultivates a sense of trust among team members towards both the manager and the organization.

When offering feedback, it is essential to tailor comments to the specific actions, ensuring they are positive and conducive to improvement. Even when addressing mistakes, the team leader should begin by highlighting any positive aspects before delving into constructive criticism. Critiques should aim to assist the employee rather than discourage or belittle. Harsh and destructive criticism can have detrimental effects on morale, potentially impacting the entire team negatively.

It is crucial to direct criticism toward the *action* rather than the *individual* responsible. Judgment should never be cast on the person while evaluating their work.

Simultaneously, the team leader should recognize and acknowledge talent and efficiency, providing due credit to team members for their achievements and accomplishments.

Problems Solving & Decision Making:
Challenges invariably emerge within a team's operations. Beyond conflicts, daily issues may surface, demanding prompt and efficient resolution to maintain workflow harmony. A proficient team manager must adeptly identify and preempt these problems, ensuring swift and effective solutions. Evaluation and implementation of remedies should be expedited, with collaborative input sought from team members.

Decision-making stands as another pivotal responsibility for a team leader. Often, decisions must be made based on available facts, weighing alternatives and considering viable options. A thorough assessment of the situation's pros and cons precedes any decision. The organization's goals, vision, and values should consistently guide a team leader's decision-making process. While some decisions may necessitate an authoritative stance, others may require collaboration with the team. Nevertheless, the ultimate accountability for decisions squarely rests on the shoulders of the team manager.

Miscellaneous skills: It is evident that for a team manager to be effective, organizational skills are crucial both in personal work and within their profession. Team managers often find themselves juggling multiple tasks and deadlines, necessitating the ability to motivate their team towards organizational goals. Proficiency in **time management, organizational aptitude**, and the ability to efficiently handle workflows, schedules, projects, and task assignments are essential.

Furthermore, effective delegation and **task prioritization** are key aspects of a manager's role. **Creativity** also stands out as a necessary skill for a manager. **Strategic planning** and adept oversight of operations are vital, including resource allocation for projects and ensuring cost-effective outcomes. The implementation of organizational strategies falls within the manager's responsibilities. Being **open and transparent** are additional traits of a good team leader, one who attributes success to the entire team rather than seeking individual credit.

In contrast to management, a team manager focuses on day-to-day task and project execution, contributing significantly to the organization's success. The team manager's essential skills play a pivotal role in accomplishing tasks that align with the goals set by the organization's management, thus contributing to overall success.

In conclusion, effective team management is the cornerstone of organizational success, fostering collaboration, and harnessing the diverse strengths of individual team members. As we wrap up this chapter on team management, it's crucial to recognize that a well-led team not only achieves goals but also cultivates a positive work culture that propels the entire organization forward. To sum up our exploration of team management, remember that empowering your team with trust, clear communication, and support lays the foundation for sustained success and employee satisfaction. In closing, the art of team management requires a delicate balance of leadership, empathy, and adaptability to navigate the dynamic challenges of the modern workplace. As we conclude this chapter, let's reflect on the pivotal role of a manager in fostering a cohesive team, where each member feels valued, motivated, and empowered to contribute their best to the collective journey of success.

"Teamwork is the secret that makes common people achieve uncommon results" - Ifeanyi Enoch Onuoha

----

3. Streamlining Team Discussions - MASTERING MEETINGS

"Meetings without an agenda are like a restaurant without a menu." Susan B. Wilson.

Meetings play a crucial role in various organizations, including business enterprises, manufacturing industries, and healthcare organizations. They serve as a platform for exchanging information, making decisions, and collaborating. Unfortunately, many meetings end up being unproductive, resulting in frustration and apathy among participants. Consequently, meetings are deemed a necessary but often challenging aspect of modern management. It is essential to understand when, why, and how to conduct efficient and effective meetings to enhance organizational productivity.

In the corporate sector of the UK, some intriguing facts about meetings have surfaced. According to a survey, employees spend an average of 13 days per year attending meetings, while executives dedicate over two days a week to prepare for them. Surprisingly, only 11% of meetings are genuinely considered productive, yet employees spend nearly 15% of their working hours in meetings. Additionally, 39% of meeting attendees admit to dozing off during meetings, and approximately 70% engage in other tasks while attending.

Considering these facts, it is imperative to carefully plan and organize meetings. The landscape of meetings has evolved due to the COVID-19 pandemic and the widespread adoption of digital technology, leading to the emergence of three main types of meetings: *face-to-face*, *totally remote* (where all participants join via a digital platform in a virtual meeting room), and *hybrid meetings* (a combination of remote and face-to-face interactions).

TIPS FOR AN EFFECTIVE MEETING.

When organizing a meeting, it is crucial for the convener to be cognizant of key factors that contribute to its effectiveness and productivity. Several aspects merit consideration during the planning of a meeting.

Purpose: The foremost consideration is the necessity of the meeting. Why is it being convened? A specific purpose must underlie the decision to hold a meeting, and its objectives need to be both clear and well-defined. It is imperative to inform the attending members of the meeting's objective. Convening a meeting solely to convey information often results in a futile effort, as such information could easily be communicated through email, telephone, or a memo.

Agenda: Every meeting requires a clear and purposeful agenda, which must be provided to members in advance. This allows them to prepare for discussion and actively contribute to decisions. Discouraging last-minute alterations and additions to the agenda is essential. Members should bring relevant data, updates, and be ready to address potential queries during the meeting.

An agenda functions as a roadmap for the meeting, ensuring it stays on track and avoids unnecessary diversions. It should prioritize topics in order of importance, allocating specific time for each and outlining expected results.

The meeting chairperson is responsible for adhering to the agenda, avoiding straying from topics, and maintaining the scheduled time for discussions. Members are also expected to manage their time effectively when presenting their input.

Participants: In a meeting, it is essential to carefully choose attendees based on their roles within the organization and the potential contributions they can make to the meeting. Including all members of a team or department without considering their relevance to the agenda is counterproductive. Only individuals with key roles and the ability to contribute meaningfully to discussions and decision-making should be invited. The presence of unnecessary participants often leads to distractions, ultimately undermining the efficiency of the meeting.

Preparation: Meeting attendees are expected to arrive adequately prepared. In advance, participants should receive relevant data, reports, or statistics required for engaging in discussions. Encouraging the contribution of original ideas and solutions to problems is crucial for ensuring active involvement.

Discussion: Keep discussions concise given time constraints. If further discussions are necessary, schedule them for a later time post-meeting. Aim for specific conclusions and decisions in discussions. Whenever possible, ask open-ended questions during meetings. Assign each decision's responsibilities to a specific member accountable for implementation.

Provide deadlines for task completion, and document these for proper follow-through.

Communication: In meetings, discussions should be open and impartial. Participants share ideas, perspectives, problems, and solutions in an encouraging environment. Active participation and input from everyone are promoted. Discussions should be open-minded and free from resentment, fostering the ability to *'disagree without being disagreeable.'* If challenging a statement or decision, the focus should be on challenging the idea, not the person presenting it. Politeness and mutual respect must be maintained during debates. Every participant should have an opportunity to speak and express their views in a meeting. Some members may be hesitant to speak; hence, the chairman should specifically invite them to share their views before concluding the meeting. No single person or a small group should dominate the discussions in a meeting.

Time Management: In meetings, it is essential to adopt an efficient time management strategy. Members should be mindful not to surpass the allocated time for discussions. The meeting's chairman should act as the timekeeper, preventing deviations from the main agenda and ensuring the effective use of time. Punctuality is crucial, and the meeting should consistently commence and conclude on schedule. Discouraging the habit of waiting for latecomers is important. Starting meetings promptly encourages attendees to arrive on time. If a meeting extends beyond the anticipated duration, a brief break of 5-10 minutes may be granted for refreshments.

Conclusion: At the end of the meeting, the chairman preferably summarizes the discussed points and decisions. A brief review of the roles and tasks assigned to each member is conducted, and deadlines are confirmed. Any outstanding questions are addressed.

The meeting concludes with a clear directive for necessary steps and actions to be taken.

Minutes of the Meeting: The recording of meeting minutes is assigned to a member acting as the scribe. Discussions and conclusions are succinctly documented, and the minutes are ideally distributed to members on the same day, but no later than 24 hours. Clearly delineating tasks, responsibilities, and their respective deadlines, the minutes serve as a reference. Additionally, they are shared with absent members for their awareness.

MEETING ETIQUETTE – ESSENTIAL GUIDELINES

Every meeting demands adherence to common etiquette, and it's prudent to bear these principles in mind when orchestrating one. The following tips delve into some of these essential considerations:

- Ground rules are typically established for each meeting, with the chairman or the designated meeting leader usually making these decisions.
- It is imperative to dispatch meeting invitations well in advance to all participants. This affords them ample time to prepare and collect any necessary resources for their presentations. The invitation should clearly articulate the meeting's purpose and agenda.
- Meetings ought to be scheduled at a time that is mutually agreeable and convenient. Holding meetings late in the day or just before lunch break is discouraged.

- Encouraging members to engage in note-taking and active listening during the meeting is essential. These practices contribute significantly to the ensuing discussion and the subsequent implementation of decisions.
- The use of smartphones during meetings is discouraged, as checking messages or emails on one's phone can be a distracting behavior that should be avoided.
- Member introductions are appropriate when the meeting is convened for the first time or when new members join. It is essential to introduce a new member to others before the meeting commences.
- Audio-visual equipment should undergo testing to ensure optimal functionality before the meeting begins. Additionally, checking the internet connection is crucial to prevent any potential embarrassment during the meeting.
- Post-meeting, it is advisable to seek feedback from members regarding the duration, content, timing, effectiveness, and overall conduct of the meeting. This feedback is valuable for organizing future meetings.
- For brief meetings, considering "stand-up meetings" is a viable option. One advantage is that members can avoid lengthy discussions while standing, promoting efficiency in communication.
- Assigning timekeeping and note-taking responsibilities to different members for each meeting ensures the active involvement of all members.
- Arriving five minutes early is recommended, setting a positive tone for the meeting and

providing an opportunity to acquaint oneself with fellow members.

- Appropriate attire is essential for maintaining the meeting's decorum; attending a formal meeting disheveled or in casual clothes is discouraged, especially in online settings.
- Interrupting speakers during a meeting is frowned upon as poor etiquette; waiting for an appropriate chance to speak is advised.
- Keeping questions and statements brief is encouraged to save time. Additionally, avoiding the use of "*you*" talk is essential, as it is considered rude.
- R.S.V.P. (Répondez s'il vous plaît – French) is commonly requested in meeting invites. If unable to attend, declining with a reason is considered polite.
- Side conversations or comments should be avoided during professional meetings to maintain the meeting's flow and focus.

REMOTE AND HYBRID MEETINGS

Until recently, the predominant form of meetings involved face-to-face interactions. However, the surge in digital technology in recent years, coupled with the onset of the pandemic, has underscored the significance of **Remote** and **Hybrid** meetings. Remote meetings, also referred to as Virtual Meetings, occur when individuals in disparate locations connect online utilizing audio and video technology.

Platforms like *Zoom, Skype, Google Meet, Microsoft Teams,* and other digital solutions facilitate hosting these meetings. On the other hand, a Hybrid Meeting involves a mix of in-person and remote participants. Both these meeting formats have rapidly gained traction in organizational management globally and are widely adopted.

Advantages of Remote and Hybrid Meetings

Let's explore the benefits of virtual meetings.
- Web conferencing is now widely used in business, training, and education across various organizations. The primary advantage lies in the flexibility of scheduling these meetings at any

time and from any location, allowing individuals worldwide to participate.

- Flexibility is a key aspect, granting participants the choice of how they attend. This indirectly supports a better work-life balance.
- Cost-effectiveness is another crucial aspect, particularly as attendees from remote locations can partake without the need for travel, saving both time and money. Additionally, organizations save on travel and accommodation expenses for participants.
- Virtual meetings facilitate seamless information sharing and enhance interaction among participants.
- Timesaving is a significant advantage, recognizing that time is a valuable resource for entrepreneurs and organizations. This efficiency minimizes the necessity for extensive business trips.
- The distribution of hard copies for relevant paperwork is unnecessary, as these documents can be digitally shared during remote meetings.
- Attendance is actively promoted in both remote and hybrid meetings, enabling participants to join from their homes or other remote locations, even when absent from the office. This fosters their active involvement and engagement in the meetings.
- Such meetings tend to be less stressful for participants, cultivating a professional yet relaxed atmosphere.
- Hybrid meetings, avoiding the need for travel to the workplace, align with green initiatives aimed at reducing the carbon footprint and emissions, making them an eco-friendly approach to conducting meetings.

- These meetings promote collaboration and innovation by facilitating interaction among team members in different locations, encouraging the sharing of views and fostering creativity and the generation of new ideas.

Disadvantages of Virtual Meetings

Like any emerging technology, virtual meetings come with their share of drawbacks. Let's briefly examine some of the unfavorable aspects associated with these meetings.

- <u>Limited Personal Contact</u>: In virtual meetings, the opportunity for personal contact is often constrained compared to face-to-face interactions. The nuanced discussions and interpersonal exchanges that naturally unfold during and after in-person meetings may be overlooked in virtual settings. Facial expressions and body language, integral components of communication, tend to be absent, leading to a potential loss of subtle non-verbal cues from the speakers.

- <u>Technical Requirements:</u> Effective participation in virtual meetings requires good quality equipment and a reliable internet connection from all participants' locations. Without these essentials, the success of the meeting is uncertain.

- <u>Security Concerns:</u> Virtual meetings are susceptible to hacking, a persistent challenge in the digital realm. This poses a threat to the confidentiality of the discussions, a critical consideration in business and healthcare settings where patient information must be safeguarded.

- <u>Technological Glitches:</u> Technical issues with internet connections and equipment may arise during virtual meetings, impacting their overall effectiveness.
- <u>Limited Social Interaction:</u> The absence of social contact during virtual meetings can be a significant disadvantage, especially in certain circumstances. Establishing and nurturing relationships becomes challenging in this setting.
- <u>Motivational Challenges:</u> Participants often exhibit better motivation when attending meetings in person. Surprisingly, an overwhelming 80% of executives in a survey expressed a preference for in-person meetings, highlighting the potential motivational disparity between virtual and physical attendance.

Requirements for an Effective Virtual Meeting

To conduct a virtual meeting effectively, certain mandatory requirements must be considered. It is worth discussing some of them. Let's delve into them briefly.

- Audio-Video (AV) technology stands as the pivotal factor in a successful virtual meeting. The equipment should meet standardized specifications and maintain exemplary quality to yield optimal results. Attendees must have clear visibility and audibility, ensuring seamless communication. Individuals in remote locations should be able to identify the speaker, fostering a comprehensive meeting experience.
- The meeting venue must be conducive to virtual interactions, particularly vital in hybrid meetings involving remote participants. Opting for a long

narrow room may prove disadvantageous, as the microphone, placed at the head of the table, might only capture the voice of the person closest to it. This setup could lead to those at the table's end being inaudible to remote attendees. Consequently, an adequately spacious room is preferable, equipped with multiple microphones and cameras. For hybrid meetings in rectangular rooms, positioning the screen on the wide wall enhances visibility.

- Hybrid meetings may benefit from a Remote Facilitator, especially when aiding remote attendees. A team member attending the venue can assist by reading charts from the screen, identifying speakers, and facilitating interaction between in-person and remote participants.

- Biases may emerge in hybrid meetings, manifested when questions from remote attendees go unanswered, and in-person participants tend to overlook them. Bridging the understanding gap between those in the meeting room and those in remote locations is crucial.

- Attendees, whether employees or personnel, may require training in handling the equipment and software used in such meetings.

- Many challenges can be mitigated if all participants attend the meeting virtually. This approach, often eliminating issues encountered in hybrid meetings, is exemplified by the widespread practice of screen sharing.

Etiquette Guidelines for Virtual Meetings

Some specific etiquettes are needed when engaging online. Several customary protocols apply to ensure a smooth and productive virtual meeting experience:

- Ensure all participants receive the meeting invite, agenda, updates, and resources beforehand.
- Arrange virtual meetings with consideration for participants in different time zones, ensuring convenience for those joining remotely.
- Thoroughly inspect personal devices such as desktops, laptops, or iPads well in advance to confirm their operational status.
- Verify the reliability of internet connections to prevent disruptions during the meeting.
- Attendees are advised to enter the virtual meeting room at least 5 minutes before the scheduled start time.
- Keep the video camera on during the meeting; it is considered impolite to switch it off while others have it on.
- Avoid eating and drinking during virtual meetings, as it is considered bad manners.
- Adhere to a proper dress code; attendees should be neatly dressed with well-combed hair and maintain a well-groomed appearance. Formal attire is advantageous for formal interviews to make a positive impression.
- Keep other electronic devices, such as smartphones or iPads, on mute during the meeting.
- In hybrid meetings, organizers should take special precautions to address concerns and queries from remote participants. Questions can be forwarded through the remote facilitator or placed in the chat box for discussion.

By adhering to these guidelines, participants can contribute to the efficiency and professionalism of virtual meetings, creating an environment conducive to effective communication and collaboration.

In today's swiftly evolving world, meetings, while unavoidable, have become an essential aspect, and virtual meetings are now a permanent fixture. Successfully conducting these virtual meetings requires significant practice, yet the time and cost savings they offer make the effort worthwhile. Regular feedback from both participants and management plays a crucial role in addressing challenges associated with these meetings, transforming them into rewarding experiences.

In summary, mastering meetings is not just about time management but a strategic endeavor to harness the collective intelligence, creativity, and synergy of a team, turning every meeting into a catalyst for innovation and progress. As we wrap up this chapter on mastering meetings, it becomes apparent that skillful meeting management is a testament to a leader's ability to optimize resources, foster open communication, and steer the organization towards a future of productivity and success.

"The longer the meeting, the less is accomplished."-Tim Cook

----

4. Nurturing Career Excellence - COACHING & MENTORING

"A mentor is someone who sees more talent and ability within you than you see in yourself and helps bring it out of you." – Bob Proctor

In the contemporary competitive realm of business and enterprise, it is crucial for organizations to enlist individuals focused on producing results and to ensure their sustained commitment to the organization. In pursuit of this objective, organizations prioritize the development of skills and employ training methods to instill motivation in employees for accomplishing the company's objectives. Coaching and mentoring serve as the dual pillars underpinning the training and growth of both the company and the individual. These approaches are essential for enhancing employee performance, facilitating their transition to new roles within the organization, and fostering success in their career aspirations. Research indicates that 70% of coached employees exhibit improvements in their performance, leading most companies to view coaching expenditures as an investment rather than a mere expense.

Coaching *involves enhancing an individual's performance, constituting a short-term endeavor*. It revolves around aiding someone in recognizing their untapped potential, leading to a sense of fulfillment for both the individual and the associated organization. Essentially, coaching centers on skill development and knowledge acquisition.

__Mentoring__, in contrast, is the process of identifying and fostering areas of improvement in an individual. A mentor, conversely, provides guidance to proficient individuals, ensuring their focus and dedication to established performance standards. The mentor's role encompasses guiding, training, advising, and fostering the career development of the mentee, making mentoring a prolonged undertaking.

Diverging from both coaching and mentoring, *__Training__ entails job-specific instruction tailored to meet a person's professional requirements.* Its purpose is to proficiently equip individuals with skills such as computing, typing, leadership, and team management. The trainer demonstrates and instructs the method for a task or job mandated by the organization, and the trainee practices it repeatedly to achieve efficiency in its application.

Both coaching and mentoring are imperative for organizational success, motivating and empowering employees to attain greater achievements in their objectives. Now, let's delve into a more detailed discussion of these two aspects.

COACHING

The International Coach Federation has defined coaching as "*Partnering with clients in a thought provoking and creative process that inspires them to maximize their personal and professional potential.*" It is the collaborative engagement with clients in a thought-provoking and creative process, aiming to inspire them to maximize both their personal and professional potential. Meanwhile, the Business Dictionary characterizes a coach as a *seasoned and reliable advisor.*

Though coaching is commonly associated with sports, its significance extends beyond the athletic realm, reaching into the business and healthcare sectors. In these areas, future leaders require effective training and guidance to attain success and fulfill their goals. A coach comprehends an individual's strengths, working to enhance them, while also identifying and addressing weaknesses with the goal of elimination. Consequently, coaching stands apart from mere instructing, offering a customized approach tailored to the unique needs of the coachee.

When is coaching necessary?

Coaching becomes imperative when an individual seeks to acquire a new skill, whether in sports, within an organization, in business, or within the healthcare sector. It is equally essential for those falling short of expectations, requiring assistance in achieving set goals. In instances where significant organizational changes occur, such as the development and implementation of a new software for patient data management and electronic medical records in a hospital, coaching is indispensable for all employees.

The need for coaching arises when there is a necessity to modify the behavior of an individual or a group of employees, particularly in sectors like healthcare where soft skills are crucial. For specific individuals within an organization, such as top management, individualized coaching becomes vital during the implementation of substantial organizational changes, like the introduction of advanced technologies. Whether the coach is an internal expert or an external professional, their role is pivotal in facilitating effective skill development and adaptation.

Skills Required for Effective Coaching

There are several essential skills that a coach must possess to effectively guide and support their proteges. Let's explore these skills briefly.

- Expertise in the subject being coached is imperative. Whether coaching a sports team or instructing a group in the utilization of new software within an organization, a coach should be well-versed in the relevant field. Imparting soft skills to receptionists or customer relations personnel also demands specialized expertise. Coaches may emerge from diverse sectors such as sports, business, psychology, and more.
- The coach must possess the ability to discern the strengths and weaknesses of the individual they are coaching, adapting their approach accordingly. The coaching methodology should be tailored to suit the specific needs of each individual, recognizing that a 'one-size-fits-all' approach is inadequate.
- Flexibility and empathy are crucial attributes for a coach. They should be able to adjust their coaching strategies based on the attitudes and personality of the person being coached.
- A coach must possess several essential qualities for effective coaching, including being a proficient communicator, an engaged listener, adaptable, patient, and adept at problem-solving.
- Furthermore, the coach should promptly provide guidance to the protégé on how to approach challenges, avoiding prolonged contemplation.
- It is crucial for the coach to facilitate the coachee's understanding of their own shortcomings and identify areas requiring corrective measures.
- The synergy between the coach and the individual being coached is vital, fostering a mutually

beneficial relationship essential for effective coaching.

- The coach needs the capability to inspire and motivate the protégé, fostering dedication, focus, and hard work to attain challenging goals.
- Additionally, the coach should instill confidence in the coachee, thereby enhancing performance.
- Effective questioning, using prompts like 'What' and 'How to,' encourages the coachee to contemplate and seek answers independently.
- Every coaching session concludes with a discussion on the next steps to be taken, ensuring continuous progress in the coaching journey for both the coach and the protégé.

Types of Coaching

Coaching comes in various forms, depending on the approach employed. [8]. Let's explore these four types briefly:

1. **Query-Based Coaching:** In this approach, the coach poses multiple questions to the coachee, guiding them to discover the answers on their own. Instead of directly providing solutions, the coach encourages independent problem-solving.
2. **Hands-On Coaching:** Here, the coach demonstrates the optimal way to handle a problem or situation, motivating the individual to attempt it independently.
3. **Intervention Coaching:** In this type, the coach observes as the coachee attempts to address a challenge or solve a problem. Only if the protégé struggles, the coach steps in, offering suggestions and guidance.

4. **Guidance Coaching:**   Typically applied to diligent and self-motivated individuals, this approach grants them autonomy. The coach serves as a catalyst, offering motivation and encouragement while allowing the coachee to make decisions independently.

MENTORING

Unlike coaching, mentoring is a prolonged process. According to Business Dictionary.com, mentoring is "*an employee training system in which a senior or more experienced individual (the mentor) is designated to serve as an advisor, counselor, or guide to a junior or trainee. The mentor bears the responsibility of providing support and feedback to the individual under their guidance.*" Mentors, typically seasoned professionals within an organization, may come from various fields such as industry, banking, healthcare, manufacturing, politics, or other enterprises. They possess expertise in their specific domain, making them suitable mentors for junior colleagues. *The mentor imparts knowledge, skills, and experience to assist another person's development and growth* [1].

Mentoring is applicable across diverse organizations. In the healthcare sector, mentoring programs cater to doctors, nurses, paramedics, and healthcare administrators. This form of mentorship is characterized by long-term relationships built on personal contact and trust. The mentor plays a crucial role in the mentee's personal and professional development, sharing invaluable experiences and grooming them for advancement within the organization.

When is a Mentor Needed?

Mentors play a crucial role in motivating talented individuals within an organization, guiding them towards focusing on their career and development. This preparation is essential for ascending to higher positions in the organizational hierarchy. Additionally, mentors are essential for inspiring intelligent employees to attain loftier goals and achieve success in their careers. Their role extends to training individuals to embrace leadership roles within the organization, facilitating the transfer of accumulated experience and knowledge to junior professionals.

The mentoring process often serves as a stepping stone to succession planning within the organization. For example, in a hospital setting, a highly skilled young physician may receive guidance from the department chief, preparing them to assume leadership of the department upon the chief's retirement.

Skills Required for Effective Mentoring

Being a mentor doesn't demand specific qualifications; instead, it necessitates certain skills to effectively guide a junior. Here are essential skills for effective mentoring:

- Expertise: A mentor should be an experienced professional in their field. Their extensive knowledge and years of experience serve as the foundation for guiding and advising the mentee, propelling their career development.
- Interpersonal and Relationship Building Skills: These skills are crucial for a mentor to successfully guide their protégé. A genuine desire to assist others is vital, and the mentor should approach the mentee with an open mind, fostering a strong relationship.

- **Long-term Commitment:** Mentorship is a dedicated, long-term commitment, distinguishing it from coaching. The mentor guides the mentee on a prolonged journey, focusing on holistic development rather than just skill enhancement.

- **Establishing Rapport:** A successful mentor establishes rapport with the mentee from the beginning. This not only fosters a positive relationship but also instills new behaviors and attitudes in the mentee, contributing to their overall development.

- The mentor should strive to motivate and inspire the protégé throughout the mentoring process, guiding and encouraging them to excel in their ventures.

- It is crucial for the mentor to be well-versed in the goals and aspirations of the mentee, working in conjunction with them to bring these aspirations to fruition.

- Mutual trust is pivotal in the relationship between mentor and mentee. The mentor refrains from being judgmental and instead leads with help and advice.

- While providing overall supervision, the mentor avoids micromanaging or being domineering.

- All necessary resources, information, and skills are offered to the mentee, allowing them space for independent learning and growth without interference.

- The mentor remains consistently available for the mentee, with no fixed time or place for mentoring. It is a continuous, seamless, non-directive, and non-evaluative process.

- Essential soft skills for every mentor include good communication, active listening, the ability to give feedback, empathy, and exhibiting a positive attitude in the mentoring process.

- The mentoring style is often informal, with the mentor acting as a role model. It is typically the mentee who chooses the mentor, not the other way around or as dictated by the organization.

- Constructive, non-judgmental criticism is provided by the mentor to improve the overall outlook and performance of the mentee. Anecdotes from personal experiences are shared to encourage and motivate the protégé. Regular meetings strengthen the relationship and offer assistance whenever possible.

- The mentor refrains from offering false assurances, prioritizing trust and honesty. Clear expectations and boundaries are set.

Expectations for a Mentee

- In the realm of mentoring, several norms guide the conduct of a mentee, and it is imperative to comprehend and adhere to them:

- Recognize that the mentoring journey lacks shortcuts; it is a prolonged and challenging process. The onus lies on the mentee to extract maximum benefits from this relationship.
- Dispel any notions of receiving preferential treatment from the mentor.
- Abandon the anticipation of immediate problem-solving by the mentor or the expectation that the mentor will single-handedly tackle all challenges. It falls upon the mentee to address their own issues, seeking guidance or advice when necessary.

- Within the shared organizational context, refrain from engaging in gossip with the mentor and avoid speaking negatively about fellow colleagues, aiming to garner favor. Maintain professionalism in discussions.
- Embrace mistakes as learning opportunities. The mentee should actively seek coaching and training to enhance specific skills pertinent to their role within the organization.
- Foster trust and transparency in the mentor-mentee relationship. View criticism and feedback from the mentor as constructive input, accepting it with a positive mindset.
- Demonstrate a proactive interest in self-development and performance improvement. Take the initiative to advance one's career and personal growth, discussing relevant matters openly with the mentor.
- Uphold confidentiality in discussions with the mentor, treating them as privileged exchanges.

DISTINGUISHING COACHING AND MENTORING

After exploring coaching and mentoring individually, let's endeavor to draw a comparison to enhance our understanding of the distinct roles each plays. It is crucial to bear in mind that, over the long term, a coach may also assume the role of a mentor and vice versa. In summary, the key differences between coaching and mentoring are outlined below in the following table.[9].

Coaching	Mentoring
Coaching is mainly task oriented	Mentoring is mainly relationship oriented
Coaching is short term	Mentoring is always long term
C. is performance driven	M. is development driven
C. can be evaluated and result is specific and measurable	M. cannot be evaluated or measured
Coaches are often paid to coach	Mentors are non-paid and do it out of largesse of their minds
C. can be independent and brought from outside the organization	Mentors are often part of the system and in the organization
Coach focusses on business issues and skill development	Mentors focus on both business and overall personal development of mentee
C. relies on software and online systems	M. is a face-to-face process involving personal relationship
C. is concerned with transforming behavior and skill	M. is concerned with personal transformation.
Coach needs training skills to teach the coachee	Mentor needs no specific mentoring skills. His willingness to help is his qualification.
Coaching involves structured meetings and interactions	Mentoring is more informal. Meetings only when needed.

In any organization, the simultaneous utilization of coaching and mentoring is essential. This dual approach serves to augment employee performance while concurrently acknowledging talent and diligence. It aims to cultivate certain individuals within the workforce, preparing them for elevated and more significant roles in the organizational hierarchy.

In conclusion, the profound impact of coaching and mentoring in the realm of management is unmistakable, as these transformative practices not only cultivate individual growth but also contribute to the overall resilience and success of an organization. As we conclude our exploration of coaching and mentoring, it becomes clear that effective leadership involves not just guiding teams but also nurturing talent, creating a ripple effect of empowerment and continuous development. To encapsulate the essence of coaching and mentoring, it is apparent that investing in the mentorship of individuals is an investment in the future of an organization, fostering a culture of learning, adaptability, and sustained excellence in management practices.

"If you want to go fast, go alone. If you want to go far, go together." – African Proverb

----

5. Navigating Critique Positively - FEEDBACK & CRITICISM

Everyone encounters criticism at some point. In organizational settings, superiors consistently provide feedback on our performance. Critique is not confined to the workplace; it extends to our homes, where family members, friends, and society also contribute their perspectives. No one is exempt from criticism, whether they occupy a leadership position or are a humble worker; it is a universal experience. While criticism can be painful, it's crucial to recognize that perfection eludes everyone, and errors are inherent to the human condition. Although no one relishes criticism, it remains an unavoidable aspect of life. Therefore, the prudent approach is to cultivate the ability to accept criticism with grace.

Criticism involves *highlighting a person's shortcomings without providing a solution or advice*. It encompasses the *"process of offering valid and well-reasoned opinions about the work of others involving positive and negative comments"* [1]. Within an organization, individuals at all levels must grapple with criticism. Simultaneously, managers are obligated to critique the performance of their team members when necessary, aiming to enhance their effectiveness and productivity. Offering criticism to an employee holds equal significance in an organization as commending them for exemplary performance, even though the act of giving or receiving criticism is not without its challenges.

Feedback *involves conveying evaluative or corrective information about an action, event, or process back to the original or controlling source.* It encompasses the transmitted information itself. The intention behind providing feedback is to enhance an individual's performance or the quality of the content they have produced. Positive feedback serves as a potent motivator for both individuals and teams, whereas improperly delivered negative feedback can be detrimental and demoralizing.

FEEDBACK

Feedback plays a crucial role in enhancing an individual's performance and fostering employee engagement within an organization. Effective feedback provides constructive insights on areas needing improvement and highlights faults without causing mental distress. Employees frequently appreciate feedback from their managers and supervisors. A study revealed that 68% of employees who consistently received feedback reported satisfaction with their jobs and demonstrated improved performance.

How to Provide Effective Feedback

Several key aspects of delivering constructive feedback are outlined below:

Timing is Crucial: Provide feedback promptly after an event, when individuals are receptive to suggestions and details are still fresh in both the giver's and receiver's memory.

Accentuate the Positive: Ensure feedback is positive, aiming to enhance future performance and motivate improvement. Highlight what the individual has done well, while also identifying areas for enhancement.

Specificity Matters: Focus on detailed aspects of performance, avoiding vagueness. Present a point-by-point analysis of both strengths and weaknesses, offering precise suggestions for improvement. Limit discussions to actionable items within the control of both parties. There is no point in discussing about things that cannot be changed by both the giver and the receiver.

Sequence of Feedback: When presenting both positive and negative feedback, initiate with positive aspects before addressing areas for improvement. Keep the feedback centered on performance and behavior, avoiding personalization. The feedback should focus on the *performance* and *behaviour* and *not on the individual person.*

Explain the 'Why': Clarify the rationale behind each point discussed during the feedback session. Clearly communicate the purpose, importance, and the manager's perspective in providing corrective suggestions, minimizing ambiguity.

Language Matters: Refrain from using accusatory language such as "*you*" and "*should.*" Instead of saying '*you made a mistake*', or *you should have asked* *me'* etc., the phrases, *'I think that what you did was not correct'*, or *'I could have given you a better suggestion'* would be more acceptable to the listener. Maintain a respectful and understanding tone. Avoid absolute terms like "*always*" or "*never*" when discussing attitude or behavior.

Honesty and Genuine Interest: Provide sincere and honest feedback with a genuine interest in the employee's improvement and development.

Actionable Feedback: Conclude the feedback by suggesting solutions and resources for the individual to address identified issues and enhance performance. Ensure that the feedback is actionable.

Enhancing Relationships: Effective feedback contributes to employee satisfaction and strengthens communication within the team. View feedback as a two-way process, valuing perspectives from both giver and receiver.

Follow-Up is Key: If recipients have doubts or need further clarification, offer assistance promptly. Consider a follow-up session if necessary.

Indirect Impact: Proper feedback indirectly fosters interpersonal relationships, promoting collaboration and camaraderie within the organization. It contributes to a positive work environment and enhances overall teamwork.

Receiving Feedback Effectively

Knowing how to receive feedback from a manager or team leader is crucial in an organizational setting. Consider the following key points when receiving feedback:

Practice Active Listening: When receiving feedback, refrain from interrupting and avoid the urge to justify your position immediately. Engage in active listening, understanding that feedback is provided to enhance performance and foster future development for the individual.

Demonstrate Attentiveness: Display genuine interest in the feedback by being attentive. An indifferent attitude sends a negative message and reflects poorly on the listener. Valuing and acknowledging the suggestions contributes to a positive exchange.

Embrace New Ideas: Be open to new ideas presented during feedback sessions. Encourage an open discussion, expressing your views constructively. A willingness to consider and incorporate new suggestions is vital.

Take Notes for Reference: If applicable, take notes during the feedback session for future reference. Record new resources mentioned by the giver. Reflect on the feedback, contemplating how to adjust your performance accordingly. If doubts arise, seek clarification from the feedback provider.

Follow Up: Implement the feedback or, if necessary, seek further clarification through a follow-up meeting. Prioritize resolving doubts or obtaining additional assistance before altering your course of action. Occasionally, modifications may be needed in submitted work for further consideration by your superior.

CRITICISM

Imperfection is a universal trait inherent in every individual. Within a professional setting, employees commonly find themselves subject to criticism, encompassing aspects such as their work, behavior, relationships, expressions, and overall perspective. The nature of criticism varies based on the source and circumstances surrounding its delivery. Although receiving criticism may be uncomfortable, it is imperative to recognize its significance, akin to the importance of praise. Both criticism and praise are integral components, forming complementary aspects of the same coin. *Criticism is as important as praise.*

Embracing praise with joyfulness should be paralleled with a readiness to gracefully accept criticism. Criticism, akin to feedback, manifests in either a constructive (positive) or destructive (negative) form. Constructive criticism is intended to aid personal development, fostering improvement. Conversely, destructive criticism tends to demoralize and is often motivated by a vindictive agenda.

Despite the inherently negative connotation associated with the term "criticism," properly delivered constructive criticism serves a purpose akin to well-intentioned positive feedback. Recognizing the dual nature of criticism and praise equips individuals to navigate both aspects with maturity and a constructive mindset.

How to Give Criticism

Let us delve into the dual aspects of criticism: how to provide it and how to receive it. Initially, let's explore the art of delivering constructive criticism within the workplace without causing offense. Consider the following key points when offering constructive criticism:

Purposeful Critique: Constructive criticism, akin to feedback, aims to enhance an individual's performance and rectify shortcomings. Its intent is to facilitate improvement, providing assistance and support.

Appropriate Situations: Criticism becomes necessary when an employee deviates from organizational policies, where its constructive nature can elevate the efficiency and productivity of the organization. It is also warranted when an employee's behavior is unacceptable or when one individual's performance adversely affects another's.

Precision and Directness: The criticism should be highly specific, focusing on a particular aspect of the employee's performance. Avoid ambiguity and directly address the issue without unnecessary circumlocution. Don't beat about the bush while offering criticism.

Focus on Work, Not the Individual: Similar to feedback, criticism targets the work or situation, not the individual. Preferably, use the word '*I*' instead of '*you*' to shift the focus to the situation, minimizing personalization. The word "*I*" focuses on the situation whereas the word "*you*' focuses on the person. So saying, "*I feel that your performance could have been better*" is preferable to saying, "*Your performance was poor*".

Private Communication: Criticism should be conveyed privately, within the confines of one's office or room, avoiding sharing it with other staff or team members.

Clarity in Communication: Constructive criticism should be communicated in simple language, potentially using the listener's vernacular if necessary. Care must be taken to avoid harsh words and insulting comments. . Occasionally, criticism has to be given in writing.

Highlight Positive Aspects: Even when criticizing, acknowledge positive aspects of the person or situation. This reinforces strengths, mitigating the impact of negative comments, and provide suggestions for improvement.

Balanced Feedback: While pointing out mistakes, refrain from offering undue praise or positive comments. Clearly explain the reasons behind the criticism, such as an employee's mistakes, behavioral impacts, or offensive attitudes.

Two-Way Communication: Ensure criticism isn't a one-sided conversation. Allow the recipient to explain themselves and ask questions, fostering a dialogue that builds trust and strengthens relationships.

Emotional Control: Maintain emotional composure while delivering criticism, using a normal tone and positive body language. In virtual settings, such as video calls, ensure the camera is on to capture non-verbal cues. The tone of the speaker who gives the criticism should be empathetic as the listener would also feel upset by the criticism. Hence care should be taken to avoid harsh words during criticism.

Mastering the art of constructive criticism contributes not only to individual growth but also to fostering a positive and communicative work environment.

How to Receive Criticism

Handling criticism without becoming defensive poses a challenge, but it is an essential skill to cultivate. Always consider criticism as an opportunity for growth and improvement. To receive criticism gracefully, consider the following points as valuable guidance for personal growth:

Positive Intent: View criticism as a constructive gesture aimed at helping you understand situations and enhance your skills. Resist the urge to retaliate defensively; instead, take time to comprehend the good intentions behind the offered constructive criticism.

Separate Self from Action: Recognize that criticism is directed at your performance or a specific mistake, not at you as an individual. The person offering criticism likely harbors no personal animosity. Avoid taking criticism personally; the aim is to guide your improvement.

Emotional Control: Avoid getting angry or engaging in arguments when receiving criticism. Exercise patience and prioritize active listening. Refrain from interrupting the person providing constructive feedback. Always keep emotions under control.

Seek Clarification and Guidance: Pose questions to the individual offering criticism, seeking their assistance in self-improvement. If necessary, schedule a follow-up meeting to address any lingering issues and gain further guidance.

Positive Response: Process the criticism, responding positively to it. Express gratitude if you perceive it as an opportunity for improvement. Cultivate a mindset that sees criticism as a chance to grow.

Avoid Self-Deprecation: Refrain from feeling dejected or overly critical of yourself upon receiving feedback. Understand that criticism is an avenue for improvement. Remarkably, many influential leaders like Mahatma Gandhi and Abraham Lincoln faced criticism without succumbing to despair.

No Grudges: Resist harboring resentment towards the person offering constructive criticism; their intention is to assist. If you believe you were unjustly criticized, arrange a private meeting to calmly present your perspective. Maintain composure and avoid losing your temper.

Perspective on Criticism differs from person to person. Some perceive criticism as a personal affront or insult. While we cannot control the critic, we can control our response. Success lies in responding graciously to criticism, acknowledging the positive aspects while avoiding offense.

Accept the constructive elements of criticism while controlling emotional reactions. This dual approach fosters personal development without compromising relationships with those offering valuable feedback.

A culture that embraces constructive input is the bedrock of effective management. The art of delivering and receiving feedback is not just a managerial skill but a transformative force that propels individuals and teams toward continuous improvement, creating a dynamic environment for success. Concluding, it becomes clear that fostering a culture of open communication and constructive critique is not just a managerial strategy but a cornerstone of organizational vitality, ensuring that challenges become opportunities for growth and development.

"Examine what is said and not who speaks."
–African proverb

----

6. Taming the Fiery Emotion - ANGER MANAGEMENT.

*"Holding on to anger is like grasping
a hot coal with the intent of throwing
it at someone else ; you are the one
who gets burned" – Buddha.*

Anger, a typical human emotion, is also evident in animals and birds. It neither possesses inherently positive nor negative qualities. Anger manifests on a spectrum, ranging from mild irritation to intense rage and aggression. When unbridled, anger can prove detrimental to both oneself and others, causing workplace issues, relationship breakdowns, and adversely impacting an individual's quality of life, often leading to severe health problems.

Remarkably, a National Public Radio poll reveals that 42% of respondents claimed to have experienced heightened anger in the past year compared to previous periods. When personal boundaries are transgressed, individuals commonly exhibit a fight or flight response, with anger serving as a notable manifestation of this reaction. If left unchecked, anger can dominate a person, subjecting them to the mercy of this destructive emotion.

It is imperative to debunk certain myths surrounding anger. Contrary to popular belief, expressing anger is not always beneficial, and suppressing it is not necessarily harmful. Some mistakenly view outward displays of anger as essential for commanding respect and status in society or the workplace. Moreover, there is a widespread misconception that anger is an uncontrollable emotion, a natural response to specific events. Regrettably, these beliefs lack a solid foundation, as acquiring the skills to control and manage this emotion is a crucial aspect that one must master.

ADVERSE EFFECTS OF ANGER.

It is crucial to comprehend the negative consequences of anger, transforming the management of this emotion from an option to a necessity. Anger can give rise to various problems, leading to unfortunate outcomes. In moments of anger, individuals may utter or commit actions they later regret. The emotions of anger and aggressiveness have the potential to damage relationships, derail careers, induce health issues, or lead to legal troubles.

The impact of anger on physical health is notable. Those with a short temper may experience insomnia, diabetes mellitus, and a compromised immune system, indicating the stress imposed on their health. High blood pressure and heart disease can also be precipitated in a person who is short tempered.

Mental health is not immune to the consequences of uncontrolled anger. The heightened stress accompanying anger can impede an individual's thinking capacity, resulting in a loss of rational thought. Anger has the capacity to exhaust a person, potentially leading to mental health problems such as depression or more severe psychological issues.

When unchecked, anger can jeopardize one's career. Conflicts with colleagues, clients, superiors, or management can have disastrous implications for future prospects. Regular displays of anger may diminish the individual's respect among peers and friends. Colleagues and friends may become uncomfortable in the presence of someone prone to frequent outbursts of anger.

In an organization, the Managing Director was known for his short temper, often expressing frustration for minor issues. Most weekly management committee meetings became occasions where executives faced his displeasure. During one meeting, a newly appointed executive, attending for the first time, was unfairly berated by the Managing Director. Upset, the executive sent an email to the MD, expressing dissatisfaction and considering leaving the organization.

This unexpected feedback shocked the MD, leading to a positive change. Upon the CEO's advice and intervention – a calm and sensible figure – the Managing Director tempered his anger, becoming more patient. The frequency of meetings was reduced to once a month, and the MD exhibited composure, refraining from reacting strongly to minor matters. Subsequently, the meetings became smoother and more rational.

ANGER MANAGEMENT STRATEGIES.

Let's explore some effective strategies for managing anger and cultivating the ability to keep it in check. It is essential to learn the art of controlling anger rather than allowing it to control us. Anger poses a threat to relationships, creating discomfort for friends and colleagues who may avoid the individual. Damage to relationships may hinder open and honest communication, with people hesitating to engage with the angry individual. Even children may distance themselves from someone prone to anger over trivial matters. The presence of anger can foster antisocial behavior, further complicating social interactions.

Identifying Triggers: Recognizing the specific triggers that incite anger is a critical step. Triggers vary from person to person and can range from a traffic jam or long queues to snide or rude comments. Justifiable anger, such as frustration with corruption or the rude behavior of a public official, should be acknowledged, but it's crucial to prevent it from spiraling out of control. Let's briefly examine some common triggers:

- Fatigue or hunger can amplify anger, making it important to address these triggers to control emotional flare-ups.
- Anger may serve as a defense mechanism, masking underlying feelings of insecurity, embarrassment, shame, or vulnerability.
- Underlying health problems like depression, anxiety, post-traumatic stress disorder, or psychoses can manifest as frequent episodes of anger.
- Negative attitudes from certain individuals, including colleagues, can trigger anger in the workplace. There may be some workers or colleagues who are a source of constant irritation to some individuals.
- Some people with an obsessive personality may become agitated when things aren't perfect, causing discontent and anger. But if other

individuals are not like them, it can trigger discontent and anger.

- Minor issues that irritate certain individuals, like a misplaced chair or a cluttered desk, can provoke anger, and recognizing and addressing these triggers is crucial.
- The habit of blaming others for everything and a pervasive feeling of unfair treatment can lead to anger, indicating a sort of paranoid tendency.

Understanding these triggers and working towards their resolution is essential for effective anger

> *A highly skilled senior consultant, sought after throughout the region for his surgical expertise, had one significant flaw—his unacceptable demeanor. While excelling in his work, he frequently erupted at fellow consultants, nurses and residents disregarding their reactions. His desire to monopolize operating rooms for his patients led to shouting at nurses and other OR staff if they didn't adhere strictly to his instructions. Despite being an outstanding surgeon, his attitude lacked civility. Even the Chief of Medical Services found it challenging to manage his unpredictable moods. Such behavior was inappropriate for a consultant expected to maintain positive interpersonal relationships with colleagues and subordinates.*

management. Learning to control anger empowers individuals to navigate challenging situations with composure.

Warning Signs:

It is crucial to recognize the warning signs of anger before it escalates. These indicators can vary among individuals. For some, experiencing a headache or a throbbing sensation in the head may signal the onset of anger. Others may notice a tense feeling in their muscles, particularly in the shoulders or jaw. Accelerated breathing and palpitations could serve as warning signs for a few. Meanwhile, flushing, sweating, and difficulty focusing might indicate the emergence of anger in others.

Now, let's explore a few strategies we can employ to manage and control our anger.

Learn to Cool Down:

Once we comprehend our triggers, it is essential to identify situations that provoke anger and promptly acquire the ability to cool down, preventing anger from spiraling out of control. Various methods can be employed:

- Upon recognizing triggers and warning signs, prioritize focusing on breathing. Engaging in deep breaths, especially employing diaphragmatic breathing, is crucial in suppressing the emotional response.
- Distancing oneself from the triggering situation can avert the anger response. In an office setting, leave the area for a short walk or a cup of coffee. If at home, take a brief stroll in the neighborhood. Engaging in brisk exercise can swiftly diminish anger and thwart its dominance.
- If experiencing tension in the shoulders or a headache, massaging the affected area with fingers or palms helps in calming behavior.
- Stimulating any of the five senses is another effective method. Admire a pleasing picture or nature, savor a candy to activate taste buds, listen to calming music for five minutes to alter the emotional state, or enjoy a fragrant aroma by

burning an incense stick. These activities contribute to a calm and collected mind.

- Counting slowly to ten is a recommended method that assists many in anger control.
- Pose questions to oneself, such as *"Why am I getting angry now?" "Is this genuinely important?" "What can I do to alter the situation instead of succumbing to anger?" "Why should I let this trivial situation ruin my day?"* Such introspection often helps cool down the situation, highlighting the frivolousness of the emotion.

Express Your Anger in Better Ways:

- Instead of throwing a tantrum, it is crucial to learn how to articulate one's angry feelings in a constructive and healthier manner. Always bear in mind the importance of maintaining intact relationships, without necessarily needing to emerge as the 'correct' party or the 'winner' in every argument.
- When confronted with anger in a specific situation, concentrate on actions that can rectify the situation.
- Avoid blaming the other person and refraining from delving into past grievances and mistakes.
- Cultivate the ability to forgive minor errors and misdemeanors, letting them fade away. Remember the adage, *"To err is human, but to forgive is divine."* As the saying goes, *"After burying the hatchet, don't mark the spot."*
- If you find yourself in disagreement with someone, be willing to agree to disagree and proceed with your responsibilities. Avoid dwelling on the mistake and the situation, preventing both yourself and others from misery.

- In cases where you feel anger towards a coworker, refrain from an immediate response. Inform them that you will address the matter later in the day or the next day. This approach allows your anger to subside, enabling a more respectful and sensible response. Once you are calmer, express your displeasure or disagreement in a non-antagonistic but assertive manner to ensure the other person understands your feelings.
- When angered, take a moment to think before speaking. Hasty words or retorts can irreversibly damage relationships. Instead, collect your thoughts before responding.
- If faced with a situation that consistently triggers anger, such as a consistently late husband, a teenager maintaining a perpetually messy room, or a coworker making repeated careless mistakes, communicate your expectations firmly but assertively. Give them an ultimatum to improve. Simultaneously, recognize that there are some aspects beyond your control. In such cases, it might be easier to change oneself than others.

Use "I" Statements to Express Anger:

Blaming others exacerbates situations when confronted with anger. When communicating in anger, it is crucial to refrain from employing "you" statements and, instead, opt for "I" statements. For instance, rather than asserting, "*You have made a mistake*," express it as "*I think you have made a mistake*" or "*You should have been careful not to make a mistake*." The latter formulation is more considerate and well-received. Instead of proclaiming, "*You are annoying me*," learn to articulate, "*I feel you are irritating me with your statement*." This approach avoids direct blame for a person's mistake while conveying the emotional impact it has had on you.

> *Another highly proficient senior consultant, excelling in diagnostics and patient treatment, unfortunately, harbored an unpleasant attitude. Despite his clinical prowess, his interactions with patients, residents, nurses, and other staff were far from agreeable. On one occasion during ward rounds, he lost his temper and threw a case file at a nurse in the presence of a patient. This outburst occurred because she failed to execute an order mentioned in his notes. The distressed nurse, in turn, lodged a complaint, necessitating the intervention of the medical director to resolve the conflict.*

Relaxation Techniques:

Various relaxation methods, as detailed in the 'Stress Management' chapter of Book-1, are equally applicable to anger management. Immediate relief can often be found through deep breathing, while long-term practices such as Yoga, Meditation, Tai-chi, and other relaxation techniques prove helpful in reshaping our behavior and responses to tense or irksome situations.

Psychologists affirm that altering our perception of triggering situations can be immensely beneficial, a concept known as "*Cognitive Restructuring*." Reacting with anger rarely accomplishes anything useful. Instead of accusing someone with "*You always make mistakes*", consider a more calming approach like, "*I am upset by the way you have worked on this project; tell me how I can help you do it better*." This statement fosters a soothing atmosphere. Applying logical thinking is crucial; one mistake typically does not signify the end of the world, unless, of course, it is a critical error in a healthcare setting. In such instances, where mistakes may lead to disability or death, an angry outburst seldom rectifies the error. A sensible approach, coupled with an assertive statement outlining consequences, proves more acceptable.

Some causes of anger stem from genuine problems and conflicts. In such scenarios, both parties should collaborate to find solutions rather than engaging in a blame game or becoming irritated with each other. It is essential to learn to respond when angry, avoiding impulsive reactions.

Other Strategies:

Numerous strategies may prove beneficial for different individuals, recognizing that like stress management and anger management needs to be personalized. Here are a few:

- Engaging in a conversation with someone who understands you can have a calming effect when you are angry. However, it's crucial not to 'vent' your anger onto that individual.
- Distracting yourself from the situation with a new activity, either at the office or home, can divert your mind from the current circumstances. Hobbies like painting, carpentry, writing, or playing a musical instrument can have a soothing effect on emotions.
- Self-awareness plays a vital role in recognizing the emotion of anger and its underlying reasons. Anger may actually be an expression of embarrassment, failure, sadness, disappointment, or frustration. Learning to identify these emotions and taking appropriate action to address them is important.
- Journaling serves as an effective method for some individuals. Putting down thoughts and feelings on paper can help overcome the emotions of anger and aggression. One suggested method involves writing down angry thoughts and feelings on a piece of paper, tearing it up, and then burning it, effectively dissipating the anger.

In mastering the art of anger management, leaders pave the way for a harmonious and productive work environment. As we conclude this chapter, remember that effective management of anger is not just a skill but a transformative leadership trait. The journey towards successful management involves acknowledging and channeling anger into constructive actions. In the realm of leadership, those who conquer anger empower themselves to navigate challenges with clarity and resilience. Let this chapter serve as a guide, inspiring leaders to embrace a balanced approach that turns anger into an opportunity for growth and positive change.

7. Mindful Perspectives - ATTITUDE

*"Attitude is a little thing that makes
a big difference" - Winston Churchill*

The term 'attitude' refers to an individual's emotional disposition towards something or someone, encapsulating specific feelings or opinions. Attitude manifests as a predisposition to react positively or negatively to people, situations, objects, or ideas. It can be defined as "*an individual's manner of thinking or feeling about a particular person, place, action, or experience.*" Essentially, one's response to various situations shapes their attitude. The thought processes governing an individual's reactions determine their attitude, which can be characterized by either positive or negative inclinations, significantly influencing their approach to life and circumstances. It is crucial to recognize that one's attitude often influences how others perceive and respond to them.

In organizational settings, the attitudes exhibited by both managers and employees hold paramount significance in achieving the organization's mission and goals. A manager harboring a negative attitude can act as a deterrent to the organization's objectives. Conversely, a positive attitude among management and senior members serves as a catalyst, motivating employees to exert greater effort towards accomplishing the organization's goals.

In the healthcare sector, where even minor errors can lead to disability or death, maintaining a positive and healthy attitude among workers is imperative. This is particularly true due to the demanding nature of hospital work — extended shifts, sleepless nights, attending to often ungrateful patients, and handling bothersome bystanders. The stressors in this environment can strain the patience of healthcare workers, including doctors and nurses. Therefore, it becomes pivotal for individuals in this sector to cultivate an excellent and positive attitude while fulfilling their roles.

THE SIGNIFICANCE OF ATTITUDE

A positive attitude holds crucial importance in both personal and professional realms, influencing how others perceive and interact with us. Let's delve into the reasons why attitude plays a pivotal role in life.

Workplace Evaluation: Employee performance is a key metric in the professional sphere. Those with a positive attitude not only excel in their roles but also advance in their careers, demonstrating the impact of optimism on success.

Self-Motivation and Achievement: Individuals with a positive attitude are inherently self-motivated, achieving more in their professions compared to their peers. They confront challenges confidently, showcasing resilience in problem-solving.

Client and Patient Relations: Whether in business or healthcare, individuals with a positive and cheerful attitude attract customers and patients. This preference positively influences organizational well-being, as patients favor healthcare providers with an optimistic demeanor.

Decision-Making and Objectivity: Positive individuals tend to make sound decisions guided by optimism, demonstrating objectivity, logic, and wisdom. This mental resilience enables effective management of challenging situations, particularly in professions like healthcare.

Enhanced Productivity: Positive attitudes contribute to heightened productivity. Satisfied employees exhibit positivity towards their work, fostering an environment conducive to increased efficiency.

Team Collaboration: Positive attitudes are vital for team functioning. Healthcare workers with optimistic attitudes collaborate effectively, significantly benefiting patient treatment and recovery.

Leadership Impact: Leaders with positive attitudes motivate and energize employees. Management's positive attitude fosters improved communication with staff, creating a positive organizational culture.

Stress Reduction and Well-being: A positive work environment encourages positive thinking, promoting productivity and reducing stress and burnout among employees. Improved attitudes correlate with better employee health and reduced absenteeism.

Accident and Mistake Reduction: A positive attitude is associated with a decrease in workplace accidents and mistakes. In critical settings like healthcare, this correlation is particularly significant, as mistakes can have disastrous consequences.

Simultaneously, we must remain aware that an individual harboring a negative attitude can wreak havoc in their workplace. Disagreements with colleagues and frequent conflicts are likely outcomes. This holds particularly true in a hospital environment, where a doctor or nurse with a negative attitude can breed dissatisfaction among patients. Negative attitudes are marked by a focus on problems without an inclination towards finding solutions, coupled with a penchant for negative thinking and a lack of self-confidence. The influence of a negative attitude extends to other team members, as individuals in such a mindset tend to believe in "*cannot*," in contrast to their positive attitude counterparts who believe in "*can*."

Within a hospital, the paramount concern is patient safety, involving doctors, nurses, and all healthcare professionals. The establishment of a robust hospital safety culture is essential to prevent untoward incidents. Patient safety is intricately tied to the attitudes, beliefs, perceptions, and competencies of healthcare workers. Notably, a study revealed that only 39% of physicians exhibited a positive attitude towards patient safety norms. Among healthcare professionals aged 30 to 35, the highest safety attitudes were observed at 48.3% [3]. Furthermore, a survey indicated that physicians generally held slightly higher safety attitudes compared to nurses or nursing assistants.

PSYCHOLOGY OF ATTITUDE

Psychologists define attitude as "*a set of emotions, beliefs, and behaviors towards a particular object, person, thing, or event*." They assert that an individual's attitude is shaped by influences such as parents, society, friends, spouse, and personal experiences. This variation in upbringing is why some individuals develop a positive and winning attitude, while others adopt a negative and grouchy demeanor.

A person's attitude comprises three crucial components, each contributing to its overall makeup:

1. **Affective Component:** This pertains to how an object, event, or issue evokes <u>emotions and feelings</u> in an individual. It encompasses their emotional response to the object or event. For instance, statements like "*I am disappointed with my job*" or "*I hate my manager*" exemplify the affective component.
2. **Cognitive Component:** This facet involves an individual's <u>thoughts and beliefs</u> regarding the object, event, or issue. It is rooted in opinions and beliefs that can be either positive or negative. Examples include statements like "*I believe that spiders are dangerous insects,*"

"My manager is a tyrant," or *"I am not compensated according to my ability."*

3. **Behavioral Component:** This component explores how one's attitude influences their <u>behavior</u>. Expressions such as *"I will not listen to my manager"* or *"I will quit this unsatisfactory job and seek a better one"* illustrate the behavioral impact of attitude.

Numerous factors contribute to the formation of attitudes, with some key influencers being:

- **Direct and Observed Experience:** Attitudes towards an object, event, or issue are often shaped by direct personal experiences or experiences observed in others.

- **Social Norms and Inhibitions:** The societal framework establishes "appropriate behaviors" for various circumstances, significantly impacting the formation of attitudes.

- **Conditioning and Learning:** Individuals can develop new attitudes through conditioning. A prominent example is the influence of TV commercials on the attitudes of young people, shaping perceptions about smoking or specific soft drinks.

- **Observational Learning:** Attitudes can be altered by observing others. Children, for instance, adopt attitudes by observing the behaviors of their parents, teachers, or celebrities. They tend to imitate these behaviors, leading to the development of particular attitudes.

Behavior and Attitudes

Attitudes exert a profound influence on individuals' behavior, with the manifestation of either positive or negative attitudes corresponding to distinct behavioral traits.

A person harboring a <u>Positive attitude</u> typically exhibits cheerfulness, a willingness to assist others, and an openness to understanding different perspectives. Such individuals refrain from unwarranted criticism, valuing the opinions of others and demonstrating a readiness to adapt their ideas and behaviors in the face of constructive criticism. They embrace inspiration and often serve as a source of motivation for others. Complaining is not in their nature, and they approach encounters with consideration. Responsibility is a key tenet for them, as they neither make excuses for mistakes nor shy away from accountability. A person with a positive attitude is characterized by a breadth of interests.

In stark contrast, an individual with a <u>Negative attitude</u> adopts an opposing stance. Such a person is resistant to understanding others' viewpoints, maintaining a pessimistic outlook on life. Self-interest prevails, and attempts are made to impose personal views on others. Criticism is a common behavior, with a tendency to attribute lapses to external factors. Acceptance of advice is infrequent, and a reluctance to change is evident. Smiling and cheerfulness are rare occurrences, with "grouchy" aptly describing their demeanor.

Another senior consultant displayed a penchant for insulting and ridiculing patients over trivial matters or comments. On one occasion, a parent sought consultation for their adolescent son, who wished to inquire about the removal of a nevus on his face. In response, the consultant erupted into mocking laughter, derisively questioning the boy if he aspired to be a Hollywood star. The tone employed was so demeaning that both the boy and his parent promptly left the clinic, subsequently filing a complaint against the consultant.

WAYS TO IMPROVE YOUR ATTITUDE

Individuals possess unique attitudes towards objects, people, events, and work. Recognizing and, if necessary, enhancing one's attitude, particularly if it tends towards negativity, holds significant importance. Here are some practical tips for cultivating a positive attitude:

Self-awareness: Begin by understanding your own attitude, analyzing yourself, and identifying potential weaknesses.

Accountability: Acknowledge and apologize for any problems with your attitude, demonstrating humility when needed.

Identifying Triggers: Be aware of circumstances or matters that disturb and provoke a negative attitude in us, actively working to manage them.

Avoiding Blame: Refrain from blaming, complaining, or criticizing others for your own mistakes and errors.

Practicing Patience: Cultivate patience in interactions, especially with colleagues, family, and society.

Thoughtful Responses: Before responding to comments or criticism, take time to think and reflect, avoiding impulsive reactions.

Big Picture Perspective: Maintain awareness of the organization's overarching goals. Our attitude will determine our advancement in the hierarchy of the organization and we should not lose sight of this while interacting with our colleagues and senior management. Our aim is to achieve the goals set by the organization, be it a company, an industry or a healthcare unit.

Emotional Management: Learn to manage emotions and relationships, fostering a positive attitude that defines your personality.

Positive Associations: Surround yourself with happy and cheerful friends and colleagues, minimizing contact with consistently negative or pessimistic individuals.

Inspirational Reading: Read inspiring stories, affirmations, and motivating quotes to boost your attitude towards life.

Choosing Happiness: Find reasons to be happy, smile frequently, and consciously choose optimism to enhance a positive attitude.

Disciplined Thinking: Discipline the way you think about people, events, and situations, focusing on positive and optimistic expressions. Avoiding pessimistic terms like "*never*" and "*repeatedly*" in favor of words like "*feasible*," "*maybe*," and "*try*" is crucial for optimism.

'Can Do' Attitude: Develop a "*can do*" attitude, firmly believing in your capability to achieve with help, acknowledging imperfection as a part of growth.

Daily Reminder: Keep in mind that a _Bad Attitude, you can never have a positive day and with a Positive Attitude, you can never have a bad day_.

Attitude in a Healthcare Setting

A positive attitude holds paramount significance for healthcare workers, instilling confidence in patients with diverse problems and emotional responses. Providing comfort to these individuals is crucial for healthcare professionals, including doctors, nurses, and other paramedical staff.

Several factors can adversely affect the attitude of healthcare workers, necessitating special attention to prevent such impacts. Some employees grapple with personal issues, disrupting their focus at work and subsequently influencing their workplace attitude negatively. Stress and burnout resulting from extended shifts, night duties, and challenging interactions with patients and bystanders may contribute to a pessimistic mindset among certain healthcare workers. Additionally, difficulties and non-cooperation from colleagues can also contribute to a negative attitude in individuals.

Expectations Regarding Attitudes of Doctors and Nurses.

Doctors and nurses, hailing from diverse backgrounds with distinct circumstances and upbringing, undergo varied formative experiences. Nevertheless, there exist certain attitudes that patients and their relatives anticipate from healthcare professionals. Therefore, it is crucial for doctors and nurses to be mindful of adapting their attitudes, ensuring a favorable impression on their patients. On occasion, some healthcare practitioners exhibit a discourteous or negative demeanor, which may be rooted in their past encounters where they themselves were subjected to negativity from teachers or parents.

For healthcare professionals aiming to cultivate and convey a positive attitude, the following points, based on guidelines from the General Medical Council of the United Kingdom (GMC), can be instrumental. These guidelines, derived from a national survey [11], encompass essential considerations for doctors. The ensuing discussion highlights key facets outlined in these guidelines.

GUIDELINES FOR DOCTORS' ATTITUDE AND BEHAVIOR.

- ✓ Doctors are expected to uphold a clear demarcation between their private life and professional conduct, refraining from letting personal beliefs influence their practice.
- ✓ Building patient trust is a crucial aspiration for doctors, who should consistently act in the best interests of their patients.
- ✓ Patients anticipate unhindered access to care from both doctors and healthcare organizations, along with the assurance that personal and medical information will remain confidential and not be disclosed to third parties without consent.
- ✓ Additionally, patients expect doctors to exhibit excellent "soft skills," encompassing friendliness, active listening, and a positive attitude.

Beyond the General Medical Council's (GMC) provided guidelines, other considerations surround a doctor's attitude and behavior:

- Doctors often acquire a positive attitude by emulating their teachers and mentors. A positive medical teacher instills such attitudes in their proteges.
- A doctor with a pleasant demeanor overlooks minor errors made by interns and nurses, opting to patiently correct them rather than resorting to harsh criticism or angry outbursts.
- Embracing the philosophy of "*Teamwork makes the dream work*," an effective doctor always carries his team along to function in an error-free manner. He encourages them to do better than chastise them in front of his patient. He helps nurture a spirit of trust within his team which consists of his interns, residents, nurses and other para-medical personnel. An ideal doctor builds strong relationships with team members,

considering their personal concerns with empathy and valuing their opinions.

- He listens to the opinions of his team members like interns, residents, nurses, technicians or other paramedics understanding that his team members spend more time with the patients than he does and hence are in a better position to air the concerns regarding the patient. He never ignores or brushes aside their opinions.
- Recognizing their privileged position in society, a responsible doctor lives up to the public's trust by prioritizing the health and well-being of their patients.
- A confident and humane doctor interacts with patients with care and compassion, addressing physical and emotional concerns, ensuring patients feel genuinely cared for.
- Transparency is key as the doctor communicates disease details in simple, understandable terms, avoiding medical jargon and taking a personal interest in the patient as an individual rather than a mere case

> *A highly experienced consultant, recognized for his outstanding teaching and mentoring skills, exemplified an attitude worthy of emulation. He consistently treated his patients with empathy and genuine concern. Prior to surgeries, he consistently went the extra mile to ensure his patients felt at ease. Even post-surgery, he maintained a routine of frequent visits to the patients, and when necessary, extended his care to home visits for follow-ups and rehabilitation assessments. His dedication and compassionate approach not only endeared him to his patients but also garnered him respect from the hospital staff.*

- An ideal doctor collaborates with patients and their families, discussing treatment details and available options, working together for the best outcomes.
- Patient respect is earned through doctors who empathetically listen to concerns, offering support and hope in times of distress.
- An ideal doctor collaborates with patients and their families, discussing treatment details and available options, working together for the best outcomes.
- Patient respect is earned through doctors who empathetically listen to concerns, offering support and hope in times of distress.

These comprehensive considerations contribute to a holistic understanding of the expectations and behaviors associated with an exemplary doctor's practice

UNDESIRABLE ATTITUDES HEALTHCARE PROFESSIONALS

Patients often disapprove of certain attitudes and behaviors exhibited by their doctors and nurses. A healthcare provider who appears timid, cold, or uncaring while interacting with patients tends to receive unfavorable reactions from the patient community. Disrespectful behavior towards colleagues can also diminish a doctor's standing in the eyes of the patients. Openly reprimanding team members, such as nurses or interns, in a rude manner in front of patients is likewise viewed negatively. Patients do not hold doctors in high esteem if they provide misleading or insufficient information about the disease or treatment. Similarly, a doctor displaying a rude and callous bedside manner is not well-liked by patients.

In the healthcare sector, where even minor errors can lead to disastrous consequences, the attitude of all healthcare personnel is of utmost importance. Establishing patient confidence and faith in healthcare workers is crucial, as it contributes to a reduction in complaints and litigations against both individual practitioners and healthcare organizations. This emphasis on positive attitudes is fundamental in maintaining the trust and well-being of patients in the healthcare system.

As we close this chapter on attitude in management, remember that a positive mindset is the compass that guides leaders through the dynamic landscape of challenges. The essence of effective management lies not just in strategies but in cultivating an attitude that fosters resilience and inspires teams to achieve greatness. In conclusion, a leader's attitude shapes the culture of an organization, influencing not only productivity but also the well-being of its members. As you reflect on these insights, recognize that a proactive and adaptable attitude is the cornerstone of leadership excellence in any management endeavor. This chapter is a catalyst for leaders to embrace a transformative attitude, unlocking untapped potential and propelling their teams towards success.

"The way I see it, if you want the rainbow, you got to put up with the rain." —*Dolly Parton*

----

8. Customer Interaction Mastery - FRONT OFFICE SKILLS

"People will forget what you said. They will forget what you did. But they will never forget how you made them feel." – Maya Angelou

In any organization, whether it be a hotel, healthcare facility, factory, or financial institution, the front office and the receptionist collectively represent the organization's public face. The initial impression a customer forms about the organization stems from their interaction with the personnel at the front office. The reception desk, in particular, holds significant sway over the customer's overall experience. Consequently, the staff stationed at the reception desk must possess exceptional soft and hard skills to ensure customer satisfaction. Front office personnel serve as crucial ambassadors, contributing to the enhancement of the organization's reputation.

ESSENTIAL SKILLS FOR A RECEPTIONIST

In this chapter, let us briefly revisit some of the essential skills required for an effective receptionist. While many of these skills have been previously discussed in both this book and the preceding one in the series, it is prudent for us to provide a concise overview.

Communication:

Communication is the foremost skill that a receptionist should possess.

- The receptionist's verbal and listening abilities should surpass expectations.
- Properly addressing individuals by their names or designations without causing offense is crucial.
- If making a person wait, apologizing with a courteous *"Sorry, to keep you waiting"* fosters a sense of care for the customer.
- Speaking slowly and clearly, with a modulated and pleasing tone, ensures customer

understanding without the need for interruptions and questions.

- When unaware of an answer, instead of stating "*I don't know*," informing the customer of a prompt investigation and subsequent response is imperative. The information provided must be accurate and detailed.

- During telephone conversations, if placing the customer on hold, notifying them beforehand is courteous.

- Familiarity with prevalent dialects in the area, considering variations in customer language, dialects, slangs, and pronunciations, is essential.

- A proficient receptionist should understand and explain written material within the organization given by the management to customers if necessary.

- Being adept in multiple languages, including the local vernacular, enhances the receptionist's value.

- Maintaining a pleasant demeanor and a smiling face is vital, with careful attention to non-verbal communication that customers keenly observe.

- Writing clearly and legibly is imperative for effective communication, making written skills a key aspect for a receptionist.

- For a medical receptionist, exceptional communication skills are paramount, especially when interacting with patients or their family members.

Being Organized:

Being organized is a crucial requirement for every receptionist.

- The reception desk should be kept clean and uncluttered, with papers filed away. The computer desktop should also be orderly, with files classified and saved in separate folders. Simultaneously, the receptionist needs to swiftly locate and retrieve files or documents when necessary.
- In medical centers, the receptionist often needs to locate a patient's file when the patient arrives at the reception.
- A medical receptionist must be well-informed about doctors' schedules, availability, and appointments.
- Receptionists should be adept at answering phones and interacting with patients seeking healthcare services. Proper telephone etiquette is essential; when answering a call, the receptionist should greet the caller, mention the office name and the speaker's name, ensuring callers are not kept waiting, and important points are promptly noted. The tone and voice during telephone conversations should be pleasant and reassuring.
- Multitasking is common as receptionists handle phone calls and assist customers at the reception. Prioritizing tasks based on importance and urgency is crucial.
- They should be capable of resolving problems for customers or patients, responding courteously to complaints, and thinking on their feet.
- Given the demanding nature of their job, especially in medical reception during busy morning hours, maintaining composure is vital. Despite the influx of patients, receptionists must stay composed and not succumb to stress while attending to customers.

Technical Skills:

Technical proficiency is essential for a receptionist, who must be adept with modern office technology, including computers, copiers, and printers. Mastery of basic software applications is crucial for effective computer use, as these skills are indispensable for inputting and retrieving information in contemporary office settings. A receptionist must not only be acquainted with general computing skills but also be knowledgeable about the specific software relevant to their role in managing the reception efficiently.

In the context of the job, accurate data uploading to a database is a key responsibility that should not inconvenience customers. A receptionist should possess a fast typing speed, and in some organizations, additional skills such as billing and coding may be required. Being open to learning new techniques and skills tailored to the organization's needs is a fundamental quality for a receptionist striving for excellence in their role.

Educational Qualifications:

Educational qualifications are significant, varying based on the receptionist's specific job requirements. Particularly crucial is education that enhances their communication and interpersonal skills. In some roles, proficiency in clerical tasks, typing, and accounting becomes essential. Moreover, possessing management skills serves as an additional advantage for a receptionist.

Customer Relations:

Customer relations form a pivotal aspect of a receptionist's role. As the front office represents the organization, it must exemplify hospitality and customer friendliness to maintain the organization's reputation. The receptionist should be proactive in providing assistance tailored to customers' needs and should handle queries amiably.

A compelling survey revealed that 39% of customers avoided a company for at least two years following a negative customer experience. Furthermore, 55% of customers expressed a willingness to pay more for a superior, empathetic, and friendly customer experience. [6].

Interpersonal Skills:

A receptionist must possess outstanding interpersonal skills, fostering positive relationships with all staff, be it employees or executives. The ability to engage in effective teamwork is a vital necessity for a receptionist. Coordinating with various departments to schedule appointments for both customers and executives is an essential aspect of the role. In medical centers, the receptionist holds a crucial responsibility in facilitating appointments for patients seeking specialized care and diverse hospital services.

Being mindful of office politics, a receptionist should steer clear of controversies and conflicts within the organization. It is imperative for them to navigate the professional landscape with discretion and avoid becoming entangled in internal disputes.

Time Management:

A receptionist frequently contends with a high volume of calls and customer requests. Additionally, they may be tasked with aiding in appointment scheduling and expected to stay informed about the availability of executives and personnel across various departments. In a medical office, the receptionist might need to address queries related to diverse medical departments. It becomes essential for the receptionist to possess knowledge about the functions of various departments to effectively address basic inquiries from customers or patients.

This demands adept time management, necessitating the allocation of time for different tasks and activities. Prioritizing tasks is a crucial skill, ensuring the receptionist efficiently manages their time without excessively dedicating it to a single task, thereby avoiding unnecessary delays for customers.

Professionalism:

Every receptionist is expected to uphold a level of professionalism, particularly in a medical center or hospital. The receptionist should possess comprehensive knowledge about each consultant, including their outpatient clinic days, operating days, and days of unavailability. In instances of uncertainty, the receptionist should promptly contact the consultant to confirm details and relay the accurate information to the caller or patient. This proactive approach aids the patient, mitigating delays and preventing any negative sentiments.

In cases where immediate information is unavailable, the receptionist should offer to call back, providing the customer with the sought-after details. This practice instills confidence in the organization. In a medical setting, the receptionist should adeptly triage

Mrs. Margaret (name changed) initially served as a front office staff upon joining the healthcare facility. Her exceptional customer interaction skills caught the attention of her team leader, propelling her up the organizational hierarchy. Remarkably, within three years, she ascended to the position of Chief of Customer Service in the center. Her outstanding interpersonal relationships with patients, fellow staff, and doctors within the organization led to her selection as a mentor and trainer for new reception appointees.

patients based on their needs and urgency. Patients requiring urgent attention from a doctor should receive priority in scheduling, allowing them to be moved to the front of the queue efficiently.

Dependability:

Within any organization, the receptionist, in contrast to the back-office personnel, directly interacts with customers. In healthcare settings, where customers are patients, it is crucial for receptionists to be reliable to ensure a positive impact. A medical receptionist frequently gathers essential patient information for registration, requiring tact and patience. This task is vital for the treating physician, and it falls upon the receptionist to input these details accurately and comprehensively into the system.

Miscellaneous:

The person handling reception must address various minor skills.

An excellent memory is an added advantage, aiding the receptionist in recalling recurring customers and patients. Recognizing a person's name upon their return fosters a sense of belonging and reflects positively on the organization.

Problem-solving skills are crucial for a competent receptionist. Dealing with numerous calls or customers is common, some dissatisfied, others seeking information, and some with complaints or grievances. A proficient receptionist prioritizes these issues, attentively addressing each, lending a sympathetic ear, and resolving matters amicably and promptly. Apologizing when necessary, they must think on their feet to rectify situations.

Independently working, a receptionist should make on-the-spot decisions without constant supervisor or team manager consultation. Taking responsibility for actions, they should make reasonable decisions during their duty.

Handling cash may be required, especially in medical centers or hospitals. In these situations, receptionists must be vigilant and accurate in cash handling and accounting. Tallying accounts at the end of the day becomes their responsibility.

Confidentiality is critical in specific organizations like healthcare setups. Patient details and diagnoses are sensitive and must remain strictly confidential. It is the receptionist's responsibility to enter this information into the system without sharing it externally.

Certain skill sets make receptionists highly sought after, especially in today's trend of globalization and corporatization. Medical receptionists, in particular, are in high demand due to the booming healthcare industry. In this competitive landscape, aspiring receptionists must refine their skills to join the industry and build successful careers.

GROOMING

Grooming for a receptionist goes beyond appearance; it encompasses a professional demeanor, excellent communication skills, and a welcoming attitude, making them the frontline ambassadors of an organization. Every receptionist in an organization should maintain a well-groomed appearance, considering the following tips:

- o Men should maintain a well-cut hairstyle, and those with beards must ensure they are neatly trimmed.
- o Women should either tie up their hair or maintain a well-coiffured look. Makeup should be minimal and not overly flamboyant. If perfume is worn, it should be subtle and pleasant.
- o Beyond external appearance, the essence of good grooming manifests in how customers are greeted and attended to. A warm smile and a cordial greeting significantly contribute to creating a positive impression. A favorable demeanor and a positive attitude further enhance the overall impression.
- o The choice of attire is crucial, and it should be both pleasing and contemporary. Clothes should be clean and properly pressed. In countries like India, the traditional sari is generally the most appropriate attire for receptionists. In other nations, adherence to the organization's norms based on customs and traditions is essential.
- o Maintaining cleanliness, orderliness, and hygiene is of utmost importance in leaving a positive impression.
- o Rigorous dental hygiene practices should be followed.
- o Nails should be trimmed, and ostentatious nail polish should be avoided.
- o If jewelry is worn, it should be minimal and modest.
- o Avoiding the consumption of snacks or chewing gum while interacting with customers at the reception is essential.
- o In a bustling reception, minimize personal conversations with other staff or on the telephone whenever possible.

In the world of management, recognizing the importance of grooming for a receptionist is acknowledging their pivotal role as the first point of contact, where a polished and professional image becomes a key asset in creating lasting positive impressions for clients and visitors.

In conclusion, mastering front office skills is paramount for a receptionist, as it forms the foundation of efficient management in any organization. To sum up, a receptionist's proficiency in front office skills not only enhances the guest experience but also contributes significantly to the overall success of the managerial function. In closing this chapter, we emphasize the pivotal role front office skills play in shaping a receptionist's ability to handle diverse responsibilities and uphold the image of the organization. The cultivation of front office skills is a strategic investment for any aspiring receptionist, fostering a seamless integration of management principles at the forefront of daily operations. The mastery of front office skills by a receptionist is an indispensable asset that aligns seamlessly with the broader goals of effective management, creating a harmonious and welcoming environment for both guests and colleagues alike.

*"We are what we repeatedly do.
Excellence then, is not an act, but a
habit."* **- Aristotle**

---

9. Hands-On Management Approach –

MANAGEMENT BY WANDERING AROUND

*"If you want something you have
never had, you must be willing to do
something you have never done."
— Thomas Jefferson*

Management by Wandering Around (MBWA), also known as Management by Walking Around, entails managers strolling through employees' work areas at unplanned intervals, engaging in spontaneous interactions. Tom Peters and Robert H. Waterman popularized this management approach in their book "In Search of Excellence," [12], with initial adoption by the Japanese company Toyota and subsequent implementation by the American company Hewlett-Packard. Disney's leadership also embraces this approach, emphasizing a hands-on, informal, and proactive style where leaders regularly engage with employees in their work environment. Managers observe employees at work, address queries, discuss various issues, and assess progress, fostering relationships, enhancing communication, and ultimately boosting productivity. This approach instills a sense of accessibility, creating a more approachable and open leadership style.

While one-to-one meetings are commonplace in organizations, MBWA stands out as an entirely informal and casual process where managers strive to promptly address employee questions and workplace issues. This 'on-the-spot' management approach mirrors the Japanese *'Gemba Walk,'* where managers traverse employees' workplaces, inquiring about their tasks and any challenges they may face. Notably, in these informal encounters, employees communicate freely with managers, unhampered by the constraints of formal meetings. Such spontaneous interactions play a crucial role in building trust and faith among employees towards their managers.

ADVANTAGES OF MBWA

Like any management technique, MBWA comes with its own set of advantages and disadvantages. Let's briefly explore the benefits of MBWA for organizations:

- **Enhanced Approachability:** When managers engage with employees at their workplaces to discuss work-related matters, it fosters a perception of approachability. This diminishes any reservations employees may have about communicating with management.
- **Encourages Idea Sharing:** In this environment, many employees willingly share ideas and suggestions, energizing and motivating the workforce. Research indicates that 82% of employees harbor ideas for improving operations but often withhold them due to diffidence. Interaction in the work environment encourages openness compared to the formal setting of a manager's office.

- **Early Problem Detection:** Minor workplace issues that might not usually reach the manager's attention can be identified and addressed promptly during MBWA. Detecting and correcting these minor problems early on can prevent more significant issues later.
- **Boosts Productivity:** MBWA has been observed to increase employee productivity and performance. Simply paying positive attention to individuals and expressing genuine interest, known as the "*Hawthorne Effect*," creates a sense of care and value, motivating workers.
- **Promotes Camaraderie:** Managers get an opportunity to supervise their team in their work environment, fostering camaraderie. These interactions contribute to a positive relationship between the manager and the team.
- **Informal Coaching Sessions:** MBWA meetings serve as informal coaching sessions where managers can provide suggestions and modifications to improve task output. Managers can also offer instant feedback during these interactions.
- **Identifies Invisible Bottlenecks:** Hidden obstacles hindering performance and productivity, as well as equipment faults, may be discovered and rectified during MBWA.
- **Enhances Employee Loyalty:** Active engagement by leadership instills loyalty among employees, who feel their well-being and professional growth are genuinely valued.
- **Inspires Innovation and Creativity:** Managers, by participating in discussions and brainstorming sessions during MBWA, can inspire innovation and creativity.

- **Identifies Development Opportunities:** Through direct observation, managers can identify opportunities for employee development and training, pinpointing skills and areas for improvement.
- **Fosters Positive Organizational Culture:** MBWA contributes to the development of a positive and inclusive organizational culture, where employees feel heard and valued.
- **Deeper Understanding of Employee Needs:** Managers gain a deeper understanding of employee needs and concerns, enabling more targeted support.
- **Prompt Issue Resolution:** Issues can be promptly addressed, minimizing the potential for conflicts to escalate and disrupt the workplace.
- **Informed Decision-Making:** Actively participating in day-to-day operations allows managers to make faster and more informed decisions.
- **Increased Job Satisfaction**: Regular interaction leads to increased job satisfaction and a sense of belonging among employees.
- **Positive Work Environment:** Face-to-face interactions contribute to a positive work environment and higher team morale, as employees feel supported and recognized.

DISADVANTAGES OF MBWA

Similar to any management approach, Management by Wandering Around (MBWA) also presents its drawbacks. Some of these disadvantages include:

- **Perceived Intrusiveness:** Frequent encounters with employees at their workplace might lead them to feel like they are under scrutiny, potentially perceiving the manager as interfering with their normal operations.
- **Risk of Micromanagement:** Certain managers may fall into the trap of micromanaging employees in their work environment. This tendency can be met with resentment from employees who prefer their own approach to functioning.
- **Impulsive Acceptance of Suggestions:** Managers providing suggestions and improvement ideas might encounter a situation where employees impulsively accept them without thoroughly considering their benefits or drawbacks. This can lead to the rejection of independent ideas proposed by employees.
- **Time-Consuming:** MBWA is a time-consuming management method. Busy managers might find it challenging to allocate the necessary time for this technique.
- **Potential Ineffectiveness:** If the interactions with employees during MBWA fail to translate into increased performance or productivity, the entire exercise may become futile. The outcomes may not always align with the invested time and effort.

IMPLEMENTING MBWA

Although termed 'Wandering,' Management by Wandering Around (MBWA) is far from aimless. Its implementation requires careful consideration and diligence to yield maximum results. Key factors to be mindful of during implementation are outlined below.

Random Timing: MBWA should occur randomly, avoiding a fixed schedule. Regularly scheduled rounds at

> *Upon becoming the medical director, Dr. Soman Jacob, the then CEO, guided me to connect with hospital staff by conducting rounds. Following his advice, I started afternoon rounds, where a typist suggested a cost-saving measure. Traditionally, discharge summaries were duplicated on expensive letterheads, but the typist proposed using standard A4 paper. This simple change, discovered during my rounds, could significantly cut printing and paper costs for the hospital. The incident showcased the tangible benefits of engaging with the hospital staff, emphasizing the value of frontline input in improving organizational efficiency.*

specific times might lead employees to be guarded and prepared for the manager's visit, hindering the ability to encounter them in their usual work environment.

Informality of Discussions: Conversations during rounds should remain entirely informal. No notes or records should be maintained. Discussions typically possess a personal touch, focusing on workplace problems, minor hindrances, work status, and employee suggestions for improving operations.

Building Personal Rapport: These informal meetings foster a more personal rapport with employees, potentially unveiling unknown talents, new skills, and leadership abilities in some of the employees. Discussing personal aspects such as families, hobbies, and interests helps break the ice and create a more informal atmosphere.

Feedback Approach: Managers should carefully acknowledge positive behaviors and suggestions during rounds. Feedback, particularly criticism, should be provided privately, adhering to the principle of *'Praise publicly, criticize privately.'* Interactions should be pleasant, and managers should be mindful of their non-verbal cues.

Inclusive Discussions: Managers should involve all employees in the area, including juniors, trainees, and senior staff, addressing their problems, concerns, and suggestions. Efforts should be made to include everyone in the conversations.

Listening Over Speaking: Managers should adopt a more listening-centric role during interactions, observing more and speaking less. The atmosphere should remain relaxed, and there should be no indication of haste, ensuring the purpose of the exercise is not defeated.

Follow-Up Actions: As a follow-up to MBWA, managers should address employee suggestions, concerns, and problems, ensuring grievances are redressed. Failure to follow through erodes trust in the genuineness of such interactions. Notes on interactions and problems discussed can be made for future follow-up, but not during the interactions.

Varied Departmental Visits: Managers should traverse various departments under their supervision during MBWA, avoiding confinement to a few selected areas. Simultaneously, visits should not be too frequent to prevent employees from feeling overly scrutinized.

In the world of management, the power of presence cannot be overstated, and "*Management By Wandering Around*" emerges as a powerful tool to foster a dynamic and engaged workplace.

As leaders embrace the philosophy of wandering around, they discover the untapped potential within their teams and cultivate an environment where innovation and collaboration thrive. The journey through the principles of MBWA concludes with a profound realization that true leadership is not confined to the corner office but is found in the everyday interactions on the ground. This chapter underscores the transformative impact of personal connection and active involvement in the management process, proving that success is not just a result of strategy but also a reflection of genuine relationships. As we close the chapter on MBWA, it becomes clear that the path to effective leadership involves a balance between strategic vision and the hands-on, spontaneous engagement that defines this management philosophy.

**"You don't have to be great to start,
but you have to start to be
great."— Zig Ziglar**

----

10. Moral Dilemmas in Medicine - MEDICAL ETHICS

"MEDICINE means Mercy - Empathy - Dare - Integrity - Care - Ingenuity - Nobility - and Ethics." — Abhijit Naskar

Ethics, a branch of philosophy, is concerned with moral concepts, defining standards for right and wrong actions and discerning what is beneficial or detrimental to individuals and society. It encompasses the principles of moral values and dictates proper conduct. The dictionary succinctly defines ethics as "*the moral principles that govern a person's behavior or the conduct of an activity,*" encompassing concepts such as good and evil, vice and virtue, right and wrong, as well as justice and crime.

The term "ethics" traces its roots to the Greek word **ēthikós**, signifying a *'relating to one's character'*. Consequently, ethics plays a pivotal role in shaping human behavior.

Each profession establishes specific principles that guide its ethical framework, including the fields of medicine and nursing. In practice, the code of ethics for doctors and nurses closely aligns, given that patients are the ultimate focus, making ethical principles inherently patient-centric. This article primarily addresses medical ethics tailored for doctors but is equally applicable to nurses.

History of Ethics in Ancient India

Ayurveda, an ancient Indian science addressing health and disease, traces its roots back over 5000 years, as documented in its ancient scriptures. During this time, life was considered sacred, and codes of conduct were heavily influenced by religious and spiritual practices in ancient India. Remarkably, contemporary ethical practices in India continue to draw from these ancient precepts embedded in Ayurvedic traditions. Consequently, the landscape of medical ethics in India represents a synthesis of the best practices from both ancient and Western ethical traditions.

Bioethics, a discipline delving into the ethical, legal, and social dimensions of medicine and medical research, focuses on ethical issues primarily concerning human health. Additionally, it extends its purview to encompass ethical considerations in the use of animals in biomedical research.

PILLARS OF MEDICAL ETHICS.

Hippocrates, often hailed as the 'Father of Medicine,' introduced the *'Hippocratic Oath'* around 400 BC, serving as the foundation for the contemporary oath taken by modern medical practitioners. Central to Hippocrates' philosophy was the guiding principle to *"help and do no harm."* In the present era, ethics has seamlessly integrated into the fabric of medical practice, influencing both doctors and nurses. *Medical ethics delineates the principles guiding a doctor's conduct, both within patient interactions and beyond the confines of their practice.* It's imperative to recognize that ethical norms can evolve over time, with what was deemed ethical fifty or a hundred years ago not necessarily applicable today.

The terms *'Medical Ethics'* and *'Medical Jurisprudence'* were coined by Thomas Percival, an English physician, in 1803. In a seminal document, he outlined the expectations and requirements for medical professionals within available medical facilities, providing definitions for these terms.[11]. In the course of their practice, doctors and nurses may grapple with ethical dilemmas, and the principles of ethics serve as a guiding compass in overcoming these challenges.

The four fundamental principles of Medical Ethics, namely *Autonomy, Beneficence, Non-maleficence,* and *Justice,* are expounded below.

1. AUTONOMY:

Autonomy refers to *recognizing the patient's right to self-determination.* Every individual possesses inherent self-worth and the capacity to make independent decisions. However, these decisions should align with principles of morality and righteousness. Thus, a mentally sound patient has the prerogative to select their physician and determine the course of treatment.

Nevertheless, the autonomy principle is not applicable to those incapable of decision-making, such as infants, children, and individuals with mental or physical challenges. In upholding this principle, physicians must divulge comprehensive details about the disease, investigations, and proposed treatment to the patient before commencing any intervention. Consequently, the physician is duty-bound to obtain informed consent, convey truthful information, and ensure the utmost confidentiality.

Informed Consent:

Prior to commencing any treatment, it is imperative for the physician to fulfill the crucial obligation of obtaining informed consent from the patient. It is the physician's duty to ensure the patient's competence in granting consent. In cases where the patient lacks the capacity to consent, as previously elucidated, a surrogate decision maker, such as a parent or guardian, assumes this responsibility.

Truthfulness:

Maintaining the patient's trust demands absolute transparency from the physician regarding the diagnosis, prognosis, and potential complications. In certain Western societies, patients receive exhaustive information about their illness and prognosis. Conversely, in some Eastern cultures like India, patients may prefer that their family members receive these details. Such disclosure often occurs at the patient's request, emphasizing the patient's right to choose the extent of information they wish to receive.

For certain fatal and terminal illnesses, competent patients may need to address personal matters before the end, such as settling financial affairs, dividing assets, engaging in religious pursuits, or reconciling with estranged relatives. The physician must carefully weigh these considerations before deciding whether to disclose the complete truth to the patient.

Confidentiality:

Maintaining patient confidentiality is paramount, and the physician must never disclose patient information to third parties without explicit patient consent.

An elderly patient, admitted with jaundice subsequently diagnosed as liver cancer, was a successful restaurant partner facing financial disputes with his business associate, currently under legal scrutiny. When consulted to examine him, I was informed by the treating physician that the second partner was eager to learn the diagnosis, contrary to the patient's wish for confidentiality due to ongoing legal matters.

Despite being acquainted with the second partner and our existing friendship, I resisted his attempts to extract the diagnosis from me, recognizing the sensitivity of their legal conflict. While this presented an awkward scenario, my commitment to ethical principles prevented me from compromising the patient's confidentiality. Such ethical dilemmas are not uncommon in medical practice, demanding resolution based on the unique circumstances at hand.

However, sharing information with fellow consultants, the medical team, or other paramedical personnel directly involved in the patient's treatment is permissible. Disseminating patient details in social media or social gatherings is strictly prohibited and contravenes ethical principles of confidentiality.

Exceptions to the confidentiality clause exist. Incidents such as stab injuries or gunshot wounds necessitate informing the police. Similarly, sexually transmitted diseases and notifiable infectious diseases must be reported to the relevant authorities.

2. BENEFICENCE:

Beneficence denotes the *physician's responsibility to act in the best interest of the patient*. It compels the physician to actively pursue the well-being of the patient, encompassing actions such as avoiding harm, upholding the patient's rights, assisting those with disabilities, safeguarding against potential dangers, and extending support in times of need. These affirmative qualities in a doctor collectively define beneficence, succinctly expressing the physician's duty to promote the patient's welfare.

3. NON-MALEFICENCE:

Non-maleficence signifies the *ethical obligation of a doctor to refrain from causing harm to a patient*. This principle adheres to moral precepts, emphasizing the prohibition of actions like causing harm, offense, pain, or injury, as well as avoiding the deprivation of benefits from patients. Every medical intervention or treatment should be meticulously assessed, considering both the potential benefits and hardships for the patient. Particularly critical in end-of-life care, decisions such as withholding or withdrawing life-sustaining treatments (e.g., ventilation and nutritional support) fall within the purview of non-maleficence. The physician is duty-bound to prioritize the patient's best interests, focusing on relieving pain, alleviating suffering, and ensuring comfort as primary objectives.

4. JUSTICE:

Justice encompasses the fair, equitable, and appropriate treatment of all patients. It dictates that available healthcare resources should be distributed equally among individuals, regardless of their societal standing, thereby emphasizing the principle of *Distributive Justice*. This principle asserts that justice should prevail based on need, effort, contribution, and merit. Costly treatments should be accessible to patients in need, without discrimination based on financial factors.

Conflicts may arise in medical practice where these four principles intersect, placing physicians in ethical dilemmas. For instance, a conscious patient refusing a life-saving intervention or the withdrawal of Cardiopulmonary Resuscitation (CPR) as per a patient's request not to resuscitate can pose challenges for the doctor.

Resolving such dilemmas necessitates consideration of the circumstances, the patient's and family's wishes, and the overall situation. For example, a patient requiring mechanical ventilation for a severe neurological condition may decline consent, introducing a conflict between beneficence and autonomy. Successfully navigating these ethical tightropes requires weighing the clinical situation, patient preferences, expected quality of life, and contextual factors such as family dynamics, culture, religious beliefs, and legal implications. Negotiating these complexities is a challenging aspect of a physician's practice, demanding experience and composure.

DUTIES AND RESPONSIBILITIES OF A PHYSICIAN

When exploring medical ethics, it is crucial to delve into the broad duties and responsibilities of a physician, extending not only to doctors but also to nurses and other allied healthcare professionals. Let's briefly examine some key principles. [7]

> *Mr. John Smith (name changed), a 73-year-old with a 25-year history of diabetes, faced kidney failure diagnosed two years ago, compelling regular hemodialysis. Consulting his physician of 25 years for routine checkups, he recently made an unusual request during a visit.*
>
> *Expressing, "I have fulfilled all my responsibilities in life," Mr. Smith, who lost his wife to cancer last year, informed the doctor of his decision to cease dialysis, bidding farewell to the world. He asserted, "This is my autonomous decision; I will no longer seek dialysis from you." In this challenging situation, the doctor found himself in a dilemma, grappling with the conflict between patient autonomy and ethical principles.*
>
> *Despite the ethical quandary, the doctor accepted the patient's decision. Tragically, Mr. Smith succumbed to his illness six weeks later. This case exemplifies the intricate challenges where patient autonomy clashes with a physician's ethical responsibilities.*

• Upholding the dignity and honor of the medical profession is incumbent upon every physician.

• While the primary consideration for every physician is service to humanity, the financial reward for services rendered is only a secondary concern.

• Only qualified medical practitioners, licensed by the Medical councils of the country or state, are permitted to practice modern medicine or surgery.

• A physician should continuously update their medical knowledge based on advances in medicine and apply this knowledge for the benefit of patients.

• They should affiliate themselves with medical societies and associations and actively participate in their activities.

• Physicians should engage in continuing medical education programs organized by recognized professional associations.

• Maintaining appropriate medical records, as mandated by the governing body of the country, is essential. Computerization of medical records should comply with existing regulations.

• The physician's registration number with the Medical Council must be displayed in specified places, such as clinics, prescriptions, and certificates.

• Prescribing generic drugs and following the rational use of drugs are imperative.

• Physicians should expose corrupt, dishonest, or unethical practices in healthcare without fear or favor.

• While financial interests should not be their primary concern, physicians should inform patients of the cost of services before providing treatment.

• Physicians must adhere to the laws of the country in medical practice and public health.

• They should follow rules regarding the notification of births and deaths, notifiable diseases, cases of poisoning, or suspected deaths. In emergencies, responding to calls for military services is mandatory.

• Physicians should always treat a patient only after obtaining informed consent.

• Abstaining from unethical practices, such as advertising (except as permitted by the medical council) or receiving commissions, is essential.

A doctor is expected to trust and be trusted, establishing a mutual trust that defines a good doctor-patient relationship. Upholding the medical principles enshrined in the Hippocratic oath, taken at the commencement of their medical practice, is crucial. Maintaining this decorum and stature is their expected responsibility.

ETHICS IN NURSING

Similar to the ethical guidelines for doctors, nursing practices are also governed by ethical principles. These principles aid nurses in addressing challenges encountered while caring for patients, guiding their decisions based on patient welfare.

Many nursing principles align with those for doctors, encompassing *Beneficence*, *Autonomy* of the patient, *Non-maleficence*, *Justice*, and *Confidentiality*. Another crucial principle is *Accountability*, wherein the nurse is responsible for her actions during patient care, ensuring high-quality service.

Fidelity is essential, demanding the nurse to remain true to her promises and uphold commitments in patient care. This fosters trust, leading to positive relationships and favorable patient outcomes.

Veracity involves honesty with the patient, building trust and improving the nurse-patient relationship. Even when conveying unsettling truths, the nurse should approach with empathy to comfort the patient. *Truthfulness* enhances patient trust, while empathy strengthens the bond.

Ethical aspects in nursing extend to _respecting the patient's dignity_. The nurse's primary commitment is towards promoting the patient's health, safety, and rights. Additionally, nurses contribute to the profession's advancement through practice, education, knowledge development, and administration. Active involvement in community, public health needs, and education is also emphasized.

Globally, nursing councils have established ethical codes for nursing practice, adhered to by nurses worldwide. These codes ensure a consistent and ethical approach to nursing care across diverse healthcare settings.

Thus, medical and nursing ethics serves as the foundation for ethical decision-making in the healthcare management landscape. It becomes evident that ethical considerations are a strategic imperative for effective healthcare management. A steadfast commitment to upholding medical and nursing ethics is paramount, ensuring the well-being of both patients and the healthcare system. In the realm of management, understanding and integrating ethical principles within medical and nursing practices are keystones to fostering a culture of trust, transparency, and compassionate leadership. The symbiotic relationship between ethical healthcare practices and effective management underscores the pivotal role that ethical decision-making plays in shaping the future of healthcare organizations.

"Medicine, the only profession that labors incessantly to destroy the reason for its own existence" ~James Bryce

---

RESOURCES

1. AETCOM – Attitude, Ethics and Communication. Competencies for the Indian Medical Graduate 2018. Medical Council of India.

    https://www.nmc.org.in/wp-content/uploads/2020/01/AETCOM

<u>BOOKS</u>

1. Leading the unleadable. Alan Willet. AMACOM books. New York. 2017
2. Leadership Step by Step. Joshua Spodek. AMACOM books. New York 2017.
3. Developing Management Skills. David A Whetten, Kim S Cameron. (8th Edition). Prentice Hall. New York. 2011.
4. The Essential Manager's Handbook: Editor. Chauney Dunford Penguin Random House. 2022.
5. How to Win Friends and Influence People: Dale Carnegie. Pocket books 1998.
6. How Management Works. Philippa Anderson. Penguin Random House 2020.
7. How to Stop Worrying & Start Living : Dale Carnegie. (Reprint) True Sign Publishing house 2021.
8. 100 Ways to Motivate Others. 3rd Ed. Steve Chandler, Scott Richardson. Career Press. 2012.
9. Never Get Angry Again : David J Lieberman. St. Martin Press. New York. 2017.
10. Anger Management for Everyone : Raymond Chip Tafrale, Howard Kassinove 2nd Ed. Impact Publishers. Oakland CA. 2019.
11. The Art of Public Speaking. Dale Carnegie. (Reprint). Clydesdale Press. 2018.

BLOGS & ARTICLES

1.LEADERSHIP & MOTIVATION

1. 10 Motivational Skills for Effective Leadership : Indeed Editorial team - Indeed Career Guide. 2023

    https://www.indeed.com/career-advice/career-development/leadership-motivational-skills

2. Leadership Motivation : A Guide to Cultivating Better Leaders. Alex Larralde. Betterworks.com 2022.

    https://www.betterworks.com/magazine/leadership-motivation/

3. Leadership Ethics – Traits of an Ethical Leader : Prachi Juneja. Management Study Guide.

    https://www.managementstudyguide.com/leadership-ethics.htm

4. 10 Things you must know about Motivation and Leadership. Zipdo. 2023.

    https://zipdo.co/motivation-and-leadership/

5. Motivation in Leadership. : Knowledge Swami.com.

    https://knowledge-swami.com/motivation-in-leadership/

6. 10 Traits of a Dependable Leader : Daniel Stewart. Stewart Leadership. 2022.

    https://blog.stewartleadership.com/10-traits-of-a-dependable-leader

7. The Most Important Leadership Competencies, According to Leaders Around the World. Sunnie Giles. The CISO Resource Hub. 2016.

    https://hbr.org/2016/03/the-most-important-leadership-competencies-according-to-leaders-around-the-world?utm_medium=paidsearch&utm_source=google&utm_campaign=domcontent_leadership&utm_term=Non-Brand&tpcc=domcontent_leadership&gad_source=1&gclid=CjoKCQiA7aSsBhCiARIsALFvovymDAn2xFYCb7brxujyxzX63TYyfKSwdJiX1VBDO0rwS57LZz1xy0caAjOpEALw_wcB

2. TEAM MANAGEMENT

1. Team Management Skills for Effective Team Management. Factorial 2022.

   https://factorialhr.co.uk/blog/team-management-skills-for-effective-leadership/#:~:text=Communication%20%E2%80%93%20the%20ability%20to%20provide%20feedback,feel%20that%20their%20efforts%20are%20being%20recognized

2. 7 Skills you Need to Effectively Manage Teams. Tim Tobierski. Harvard Business School. 2020.

   https://online.hbs.edu/blog/post/team-management-skills#:~:text=Emotional%20intelligence%20refers%20to%20an%20individual's%20ability,a%20keen%20sense%20of%20self%2Dawareness%2C%20empathy%2C%20and

3. 8 Effective Team Management Skills every Manager should know. Jennifer Herrity. Indeed-Career Guide. 2023.

   https://www.indeed.com/career-advice/career-development/team-management-skills

4. 10 Examples of Effective Team Management Skills. Indeed Editorial Team. Indeed-Career Guide. 2023.

   https://www.indeed.com/career-advice/resumes-cover-letters/team-management-skill

5. 10 Team Management Skills to Start Building Today. Julia Martins. ASANA. 2022.

   https://asana.com/resources/team-management-skills

6. Team Management Skills. Mind Tools Content Team. Mind Tools 2023.

https://www.mindtools.com/a4j6oek/team-management-skills

7. 15 Essential Team Management Skills for the First Time Team Managers. Ashley Bell.   Snack Nation. 2023.

https://snacknation.com/blog/team-management-skills/

3. MASTERING MEETINGS

1. 7 Secrets to Become a Master of Meetings. Lindsey Pollack. 2023.

https://lindseypollak.com/7-secrets-to-become-a-master-of-meetings/

2. Mastering the Art of Effective Meetings : Key Inputs and Outputs. Charlie Shephard. Linked In.

https://www.linkedin.com/pulse/mastering-art-effective-meetings-key-inputs-outputs-charlie-shephard/

3. 14 Essential Tips for Mastering Meeting Etiquette. Lizz Forth. Namely. 2023.

https://blog.namely.com/14-essential-tips-for-mastering-meeting-etiquette

4. Tips for Mastering the Meeting. Meyling Ortiz. Above the Law. 2022.

https://abovethelaw.com/2022/07/tips-for-mastering-the-meeting/

5. Mastering the Art of Hybrid Meetings. Dr. Gleb Tsipursky. Disaster Avoidence Experts. 2023.

https://disasteravoidanceexperts.com/mastering-the-art-of-hybrid-meetings/

6. 10 Tips for Mastering a Virtual Meeting. Mike Prevou. Part of the SKS Teams of Leaders Approach. 2013.

https://strategicks.com/wp-content/uploads/2013/11/10-Tips-for-Mastering-a-Virtual-Meeting.pdf

7. 9 Tips for Effective Meetings. Bill Phillips. Digital Marketing Institute. 2023.

    https://digitalmarketinginstitute.com/blog/tips-for-effective-meetings

8. 12 Best Practices for Productive Meetings. Matt Green 2023. Skillcast.

    https://www.skillcast.com/blog/best-practices-productive-meetings

9. 28+ Incredible Meeting Statistics [2023] : Virtual, Zoom, In-person Meetings and Productivity. Jack Flynn. Zippia.com 2023.

    https://www.zippia.com/advice/meeting-statistics/   check this

4. COACHING AND MENTORING

1. Mentoring vs Coaching : The Key Differences and Benefits. Webinar. Pushfar 2021.
    https://www.pushfar.com/article/mentoring-vs-coaching-the-key-differences-and-benefits/#:~:text=The%20Definitions%20of%20Coaching%20and%20Mentoring&text=A%20mentor%20is%20someone%20who,them%20reach%20their%20full%20potential.

2. Know the Difference between Coaching and Mentoring. Christine Zust. Kent State University. 2017.

    https://www.kent.edu/yourtrainingpartner/know-difference-between-coaching-and-mentoring

3. What is the Difference between a Coach and a Mentor ? Nathan Goldstein. Together Mentoring Software. 2023.

    https://www.togetherplatform.com/blog/what-is-the-difference-between-mentorship-and-coaching

4. The 5Cs Model of Team Coaching. OCM Enable. 2023.

https://www.theocm.co.uk/ocm-enable/insights/5cs-model-team-coaching#:~:text=Our%20model%20of%20team%20coach,on%20the%20team's%20unique%20context.

5. How to Develop Coaching and Mentoring Programs to Develop new Leaders. Center for Creative Leadership. Leading Effectively Staff 2021.

    https://www.ccl.org/articles/leading-effectively-articles/how-to-use-coaching-and-mentoring-programs-to-develop-new-leaders/

6. Coaching and Mentoring. Mindtools. 2023.

    https://www.mindtools.com/c067tpn/coaching-mentoring

7. Coach or Mentor ? You need both. Kasey Hickey. BetterUp 2020.

    https://www.betterup.com/blog/coach-or-mentor-you-need-both

8. Coaching and Mentoring. Tutorials Point India. 2015.

    https://twitter.com/tutorialspoint

9. Coaching vs. Mentoring. – 25 Ways they're Different. by Management Mentors 2013.

    www.management-mentors.com

10. Mentor-Mentee Relationship in Medicine. Javier P Gisbert. Gastroenterología y Hepatología (English Edition), Volume 40, Issue 1, 2017, Pages 48-57

    https://www.sciencedirect.com/science/article/abs/pii/S2444382417300202

5. FEEDBACK & CRITICISM

1. Steps to Handle Criticism at Work – Indeed Editorial Team. 2023.

    https://www.indeed.com/career-advice/career-development/steps-to-handle-criticism-at-

work#:~:text=Though%20one%20feels%20much%20better,L
earn

2. How to Give (and take) Constructive Criticism. Julia Martins
    - Asana.com. 2022.

    https://asana.com/resources/constructive-criticism

3. Constructive Criticism : Feedback that motivates your Team.
    Fingerprint for Success. 2023.

    https://www.fingerprintforsuccess.com/blog/constructive-
    criticism

4. What is the Difference between Feedback and Criticism. Iulia
    Christina Uta. Brandminds.com. 2022.

    https://brandminds.com/what-is-the-difference-between-
    feedback-and-criticism/

5. Effective Feedback: Key elements to Keep in Mind.
    Lopamudra. Vantage Circle 2021.

    https://blog.vantagecircle.com/effective-feedback/

6. Receiving and Giving Effective Feedback. Center for Teaching
    Excellence. University of Waterloo. 2023.

    https://uwaterloo.ca/centre-for-teaching-
    excellence/catalogs/tip-sheets/receiving-and-giving-effective-
    feedback

6. ANGER MANAGEMENT

1. Anger Management. 10 Tips to Tame your Temper : Mayo
    Clinic Staff. Mayo Clinic. 2022.

    https://www.mayoclinic.org/healthy-lifestyle/adult-
    health/in-depth/anger-management/art-20045434

2. Control Anger before it Controls You. : American Psychological
    Association 2022.

    https://www.apa.org/topics/anger/control

3. 11 Anger Management Strategies to help you Calm Down. Amy Morin. Verywellmind 2022.

https://www.verywellmind.com/anger-management-strategies-4178870

4. Anger Management. Melinda Smith. Helpguide.org. 2023.

https://www.helpguide.org/articles/relationships-communication/anger-management.htm

5. Anger Management.   Skillsyouneed. 2023.

https://www.skillsyouneed.com/ps/anger-management.html

6. 14 Anger Management Techniques to Promote Calm. : Laura A. Maddox. Betterhelp. 2023.

https://www.betterhelp.com/advice/anger/14-anger-management-techniques-and-how-they-work/

7. 17 Anger Management Tips to (Immediately) Control Yourself. : Galina Hitching. Science of People. 2023.

https://www.scienceofpeople.com/how-to-control-anger/

7. ATTITUDE

1. Attitude – An Important Management Tool.   James L. Mazurek. Illinois Municipal Review. 1989.

https://www.lib.niu.edu/1989/im890707.html#:~:text=A%20Manager%2FDepartment%20Head%20with,personal%20commitment%20and%20personal%20respect.

2. Positive Attitude in Healthcare. Lockton Affinity Health. 2022.

https://locktonaffinityhealth.com/2022/03/01/positive-attitude-in-healthcare/

3. Healthcare Professionals' Attitudes Regarding Patient Safety. Cross Sectional Survey. Brasaite, I., Kaunonen, M., Martinkenas, A. *et al. BMC Res Notes* **9**, 177 (2016).

https://bmcresnotes.biomedcentral.com/articles/10.1186/s13
104-016-1977-7#citeas

4. Why a Positive Attitude is Essential in Healthcare. Nurse Advisor 2023.

    http://nurseadvisormagazine.com/tn-exclusive/why-a-positive-attitude-is-essential-in-healthcare/

5. The Power of Attitude. Focus 3. 2023.

    https://focus3.com/the-power-of-attitude/

6. Bad Attitude Among Doctors. Pamela Q. Fernandes. May 2017.

    https://www.pamelaqfernandes.com/qmc-9-bad-attitude-among-doctors/

7. What makes a Good Doctor? 7 Surprisingly Useful Skills for Physicians. St. George's University School of Medicine. 2021.

    https://www.sgu.edu/blog/medical/what-makes-a-good-doctor/

8. Why a Manager's Attitude Matters. Deb Calvert. People First Productivity Solutions. 2019
    https://blog.peoplefirstps.com/connect2lead/the-attitude-of-a-good-manager-why-it-matters#:~:text=Being%20optimistic%2C%20confident%2C%20trusting%2C,bringing%20negativity%20into%20the%20workplace.

9. What is Attitude? Definition, Types, Components, Formation, Functions, Characteristics. GeekToNight. 2023.
    https://www.geektonight.com/what-is-attitude-meaning-functions-types-importance-components/

10. The Components of Attitude : Definition, Formation, Changes: Cherry K, Susman D. Very Well Mind. 2023.

    https://www.verywellmind.com/attitudes-how-they-form-change-shape-behavior-2795897#:~:text=In%20psychology%2C%20an%20attitude%20refers,people%20act%20in%20various%20situations.

11. The Standards Expected of Doctors. Patient and Public Attitudes: Valdeep Gill, Sally Bridges, Carol McNaughton Nicholls. General Medical Council. National Center for Social Research. 2012.

https://www.gmc-uk.org/-/media/gmc-site/about/gmcstandardsexpectedofdoctorsfinalreportv2pdf51766111.pdf

8. FRONT OFFICE SKILLS

1. Make Your Resume Pop with these 8 Receptionist skills. Robert Half. 2023.

https://www.roberthalf.com/ca/en/insights/landing-job/8-skills-that-will-make-your-receptionist-resume-pop

2. 12 Essential and Necessary Skills of Front Office Professionals. HCareers. 2023.

https://www.hcareers.com/article/career-advice/12-necessary-and-essential-skills-of-front-desk-professionals

3. 18 Receptionist Skills that will make Your Resume Stand out. Packagex. 2021.

https://packagex.io/blog/best-receptionist-skills

4. Front Desk Agent Skills for your Resume and Career. Zippia. 2023.

https://www.zippia.com/front-desk-agent-jobs/skills/?src=chatbot_popout_displayed

5. Front Desk Clerks - Skills and Abilities. Illinois WorkNet Center .

https://apps.illinoisworknet.com/cis/clusters/OccupationDetails/100103?parentId=110900§ion=skills§ionTitle=Skills%20and%20Abilities

6. 5 Skills Everey Receptionist needs in 2024. Swipedon. Paul Hansen 2023.

https://www.swipedon.com/blog/skills-every-receptionist-needs

7. 10 of the Most Essential Medical Receptionist Resume Skills. Indeed Editorial Team. INDEED Career Guide. 2022.

https://ca.indeed.com/career-advice/resumes-cover-letters/medical-receptionist-resume-skills

9. MBWA

10. Management by Wandering Around (MBWA). Mind Tools Content Team. MindTools. 2023.

https://www.mindtools.com/a79izhx/management-by-wandering-around-mbwa

11. Managing By Walking Around. Ivan Andreev. Valamis.com. 2023.

https://www.valamis.com/hub/managing-by-walking-around

12. MBWA meaning: Tips for Management by Walking Around : Masterclass.com. 2022.

https://www.masterclass.com/articles/mbwa

13. Management by Walking Around.   Nandita Saravanakumar. Wallstreet Mojo 2024.

https://www.wallstreetmojo.com/management-by-walking-around/

14. 5 Reasons why MBWA could be your best management strategy yet. Ann Gomez. Clear Concept 2015.

https://clearconceptinc.ca/5-reasons-why-mbwa-could-be-your-best-management-strategy-yet/

10. MEDICAL ETHICS

1. The Four Pillars of Medical Ethics. Medical Protection. 2023.

https://www.medicalprotection.org/uk/articles/essential-learning-law-and-ethics

2. Principles of Clinical Ethics and their Application to Practice. Basil Varkey. <u>Med Princ Pract.</u> 2021 Feb; 30(1): 17–28.

    https://www.ncbi.nlm.nih.gov/pmc/articles/PMC7923912/

3. Medical Ethics. The Medical Portal. 2023.

    https://www.themedicportal.com/application-guide/medical-school-interview/medical-ethics/

4. Principles of Bioethics. Thomas R. McCormick UW Medicine. 2018.

    https://depts.washington.edu/bhdept/ethics-medicine/bioethics-topics/articles/principles-bioethics

5. Medical Ethics. Wikipedia. 2023

    https://en.wikipedia.org/wiki/Medical_ethics

6. Healthcare Ethics in Modern Medicine. Nursing & Healthcare 2019.

    https://www.wgu.edu/blog/healthcare-ethics-modern-medicine1908.html#close

7. Medical Ethics. Markose A, Krishnan R, Ramesh M. <u>J Pharm Bioallied Sci.</u> 2016 Oct; 8(Suppl 1): S1–S4.

    https://www.ncbi.nlm.nih.gov/pmc/articles/PMC5074007/

8. Ethics in Nursing : 10 Things to Know. Lisa Bonsall. Lippincott Nursing Center 2023.

    https://www.nursingcenter.com/ncblog/june-2023/ethics-in-nursing-10-things-to-know

9. The History of Medical Ethics in India. Angel Prabhakar. Columbia University Libraries. 2022.

    https://journals.library.columbia.edu/index.php/bioethics/article/view/10117

10. Professional Conduct, Etiquette and Ethics) Regulations, 2002 Indian Medical Council.

https://wbconsumers.gov.in/writereaddata/ACT%20&%20R
ULES/Relevant%20Act%20&%20Rules/Code%20of%20Medi
cal%20Ethics%20Regulations.pdf

11. Code of Medical Ethics as Applicable to Doctors. Dr. K.K.
    Aggarwal. Indian Medical Association. 2002.

    https://ima-india.org/windata/ccima/Legal/6.pdf

12. The Code of Medical Ethics of the American Medical
    Association. Riddick, Frank – The Ochsner Journal 5 (2): 6 –
    10.

    https://code-medical-ethics.ama-assn.org/

13. American Nurses Association. (2015). Code of Ethics for
    Nurses.

    https://www.nursingworld.org/practice-policy/nursing-
    excellence/ethics/code-of-ethics-for-nurses/

****

A Humble Request to the Reader

Thank you for buying and reading this book. May I request your indulgence for one more favor. I hope you enjoyed reading this book and derived benefit from the assorted topics discussed.

Kindly give your sincere and valuable review of this book in the Amazon site. Your rating and candid review will be a great inspiration and encouragement to me.

I would also request you to check my other books – ***Tell Me a Story, Grandpa*** and ***Grandpa Tell Me More Stories*** which are a compilation of short stories with morals, written with children in mind.

Also, the book of '***In Search of a Bridegroom***' is an interesting Autobiographical Fiction of true events.

Two books on the Health Problems faced by the Elderly are available under the names, "***How to face the Health Challenges While getting Old***" and "***Old Age Health – Challenges and Solutions***" These deal with the Health Challenges in old age, their Early Recognition, Prevention and Treatment.

My recent medical book named "***Understanding the Electrocardiogram***" is a book written for the benefit of the Medical fraternity. It is a book on Electrocardiography.

The book "***Demystifying Hinduism***" is a book describing the Basics of Hinduism in a simple manner and is Book 1 of the series '*Understanding Hinduism*'. The second book **"The Avadhoota"** in the series describes the journey of a monk in search of truth from Nature. The book "*Daily Musings*" is a collection of sixty inspirational messages for daily living.

"*How to Master Essential Life Skills*" is a book outlining the important skills anyone aiming for success in life needs.

You can contact me at my email address ramani2911@gmail.com

https://www.linkedin.com/in/sahasranam-dr-k-v-3231a13a/   (Linked In)

https://medium.com/@ramani2911/membership (Medium.com)

Thank you for your Co-operation.

APPENDIX
MORE BOOKS BY THE AUTHOR
How to Face the Challenges while Growing Old

Old Age Health Challenges and Solutions

(Problems of Old Age Series)

This is a series of two books dealing with the Health Problems faced by the Elderly. Most of the Systems of the human body and their problems are discussed in the books. Recognition of the symptoms of the various diseases of old age and their prevention are discussed. The available modalities of treatment are mentioned in brief. This is a book for the public and not for the medical profession. It makes the average person aware of what he will face when he becomes older.

Tell Me a Story, Grandpa

Grandpa, Tell me More Stories

(Children's Short Stories Series)

This a series of books of Short Stories for children. The books abound in short stories imparting morals and values which will fascinate and entertain children. Ideal for children in the school going age. The books provide excellent bed time stories for children. Each book has 40 such stories that will keep children entertained during the holidays. The books are ideal to be gifted to children on birthdays and other festivals. The books are recommended to be added to the school libraries.

Understanding the Electrocardiogram

(For the Doctor's Pocket)

A simple Pocket Book of interpreting the Electrocardiogram which can be carried during Ward Rounds and in the ICU. Interpretation of ECG is explained in simple language with more than 150 illustrations and ECG tracings.

The book is in 3 parts - *12 Lead ECG Interpretations, Arrhythmias-Disorders of Impulse Generation - Arrhythmias - Disorders of Impulse Conduction.*

Immensely Useful for Doctors, General & Family Practitioners, Medical Students, Interns, Residents, Nurses, and Paramedics. It makes the methodical interpretation of ECGs a child's play.

Demystifying Hinduism

(Understanding Hinduism – Book 1)

Hinduism, which is truly named "*Sanatana Dharma*" is undergoing a great revival in the Modern World. The Hindu Diaspora which is spread all over the world find it difficult to understand and learn the basics of Hinduism. The new generation of Hindu youth also need to get to know the Foundation of Hinduism.

This book describes the Basic Facts about Hinduism in a simple language for easy understanding. The book which is in a Question & Answer format, discusses, the origin of Religion, the Hindu Scriptures, the Idol worship and its symbolism, Rituals and Temple Worship, Yoga, Dharma, Meditation and Hindu Festivals. The Varna Ashrama system, Death & Reincarnation, and the Concept of Time in Hinduism are elaborately, but clearly described.

The Avadhoota – Whispers of Wisdom

Daily Musings – Nourishment for your Soul

(Understanding Hinduism Book 2 & 3)

The book **"The Avadhoota"** presents a fictionalized rendition of the Yadu-Avadhoota Samvadam found in the Srimad Bhagavatham. Within its pages, the author eloquently portrays the Twenty-four Gurus as originally described by the Avadhoota. The narrative follows the journey of the Brahmachari sage Datta, who embarks on a nationwide expedition to glean experiential insights into the various teachings of Hindu philosophy.

To enhance the textual variety, the author presents the chapter summaries in the form of verses injecting a rhythmic cadence that complements the overall content.

The book **"Daily Musings"** is a garland of 60 inspirational and motivational passages for everyday living.

In Search of a Bridegroom

(An Autobiographical Fiction)

An interesting Autobiographical Fiction, where the author takes the reader through the journey where he was in search of a bridegroom for his daughter. Interesting anecdotes and embarrassing circumstances are described by the author in an amusing manner and finally, he succeeds in finding an appropriate groom for his daughter. The book is based on true facts and combines moments of suspense and hilarious incidents.

How to Master Essential Life Skills

(A book on Professional Skill Development)

The first book in the series "Skillsets for Success" describing various skills needed for a Professional, Administrator, Student, Healthcare Professional or a Housewife tailored for professionals in any field. It is a book where the important life skills are given in a simple and abridged form. Anecdotes from the author's personal experiences have been added.